Table Of Contents

95275

➲   **Notice.** This book presents suggestions that may help you to reduce the risk of child sexual abuse within your organization. Unfortunately, however, no foolproof procedure to eliminate child sexual abuse exists. It is possible that an incident may occur even if you implement all the suggestions in this book. You are encouraged to review this resource carefully and to consult a local attorney to receive advice concerning your state laws and their impact upon your organization's reporting procedures and employment practices.

Every effort has been made to make the materials in this text current as of the date of publication. Laws, however, are subject to change. Such changes may affect the accuracy of this book. These changes are updated bimonthly in our publication *Church Law & Tax Report.*

CHURCH LAW & TAX REPORT

Reducing the Risk of Child Sexual Abuse in Your Church

A complete and practical guidebook for prevention and risk reduction

Richard R. Hammar, Steven W. Klipowicz, & James F. Cobble, Jr.

Christian Ministry Resources
PO Box 1098
Matthews, NC 28106
(704) 841-8066
Fax (704) 841-8039

Preface

Since the inception of *Church Law & Tax Report,* no topic has generated more response than our articles on sexual molestation and the church.

Sexual molestation in the church is not something new. Only within the past decade, though, has it become a topic for open discussion. To a large extent, this new openness has been forced upon the church through litigation and media attention. Often, an attitude of denial or minimization has existed among church leaders concerning this tragic problem. Many local church leaders still cannot believe that sexual molestation could ever occur in their churches.

In November, 1992, approximately 100 denominational leaders, attorneys, church educators, and insurance executives gathered in Chicago, Illinois, to discuss how the church could respond to this problem. Every major religious group was represented. The first draft of this book was presented at that meeting. An editorial committee was formed from the participants and, over the following several months, intense effort and attention were given to finalizing this book.

This book reflects input and feedback from church executives, denominational attorneys, insurance leaders, social workers, clergy, educators, prosecutors, congregational members, and victims of abuse.

The focus of this book is prevention. The goal is both to inform church leaders of the problem of sexual abuse, and to empower them to lower the risk of sexual abuse through preventive measures. The book is not meant to be a resource for therapeutic aid for victims. Many excellent resources and agencies exist that provide help for the abuse victim. Few resources exist, however, that provide direct organizational support and guidance to establish and maintain a prevention program. We have attempted to address that need. Our work reflects both the legal realities that churches face today, and the organizational concerns regarding program implementation.

We recognize that no single approach will work for every church. Nevertheless, this book provides a starting point that will be of value to any church or nonprofit organization concerned about reducing the risk of sexual molestation.

In addition to this book, an audio cassette tape, a video cassette tape, and a leader's guide are also being prepared to help churches establish a prevention program. These resources are occasionally referred to in this book. A complete description of each resource is found in Appendix 7. All resources should be available by late Spring of 1993.

We value any feedback you can provide concerning this book. Send your comments to Christian Ministry Resources, PO Box 2301, Matthews, NC 28106.

Richard Hammar
Steven W. Klipowicz
James Cobble

April 1993

Introduction

Child molestation is a serious problem. Molesters want to put themselves in pivotal positions where they access children. The church needs to address this societal issue. Gene Abel, M.D., The Cardinal's Commission on Clerical Sexual Misconduct With Minors (Chicago: Archdiocese of Chicago, June 1992) p. 54.

The stakes are very high on all sides. The credibility of the church rests on the church's ability to face the problem of child molesters among the clergy and remove them. For the child who is raised in the church and taught to respect and trust the authority of the clergy, the betrayal of trust that occurs when the clergyperson molests him or her is a profound violation. The child quickly realizes that the church is not a safe place. Marie Fortune, "A Millstone 'Round the Neck," Round Table, Spring 1990, p. 20.

No single pastoral problem is more painful to us as bishops than the situation of sexual abuse where the offender is a member of the clergy or is a person in the employ of the church and the offended is a child. Archbishop Daniel Pilarczyk, Roman Catholic Church, Cincinnati, Ohio.

Children have neither power nor property. Voices other than their own must speak for them. If those voices are silent then children who have been abused may lean their heads against window panes and taste the bitter emptiness of violated childhoods. Justice Francis T. Murphy in a speech on sexual abuse in 1985.

Child sexual abuse strikes children from every social background, race, and age. Often it occurs in settings where children or youth completely trust adults—homes, schools, camps, athletic and park programs, and most sadly, the church.

Child sexual abuse can happen in any church—*including yours.* A profound legal and moral obligation exists to reduce the possibility of child sexual abuse from ever occurring. The purpose of this book is to help you make your church a safer place. It will assist you to:

❏ Safeguard the children and youth of your church from sexual molestation.

❏ Protect church staff and volunteer workers from potential allegations of sexual abuse.

❏ Limit the extent of your church's legal risk and liability due to sexual abuse.

How To Use This Book

This book provides a rationale, policies, procedures, sample forms, and an implementation strategy that your church can use to create a sexual abuse prevention plan. Reflecting a unique blend of information and guidance, the book is organized into three distinct parts.

Part One: Enlistment

⇨ *Use Part One to motivate key leaders to initiate and support a prevention program in your church.*

Part One helps church leaders develop both an understanding of the problem of child sexual abuse in the church and a commitment to do something about it. The possibility of sexual abuse happening in a church is often minimized or not even considered. Part One alerts church leaders to the need for a prevention program by providing a clear picture of the *personal* and *legal* consequences of child sexual abuse.

Part Two: Policy Formation

⇨ *Use Part Two to create policies and procedures.*

Part Two examines specific policies and procedures that can be used to undergird your sexual abuse prevention plan. Attention is given to worker selection, worker supervision, reporting requirements, and the response to possible incidents of child abuse.

Part Three: Training and Implementation

⇨ *Use Part Three to develop an implementation strategy and a training program for church workers.*

Part Three provides guidance for staff training and includes a comprehensive model for implementation. An effective prevention program must rely on ongoing congregational support and the adequate training of paid staff and volunteers.

To begin, read the entire book through once to get the big picture. Then use individual chapters according to your needs. As you read the book, consider how it can be creatively used to protect the children, youth, and workers of your church. The purpose of this book is not only to provide information, but to empower you and your church to take preventive action.

Part One

Enlistment

Building Support and Commitment To Prevent Child Sexual Abuse From Occurring In Your Church

1. The Need For A Prevention Program

The Problem Is Real

Ed begins attending First Church. After a few weeks, he volunteers to work with the youth group. Church staff members do not know Ed, but they are delighted to have another worker. He is put to work immediately. The youth group has an overnight activity a few months later. Following the activity, two minors report that they were sexually molested by Ed. The parents of one of the minors contact an attorney, and a $3 million lawsuit is brought against Ed, the church, and the church board. The parents claim that the church (and the church board) acted negligently by not doing any background investigation before using Ed as a volunteer worker.

This tragic story represents an increasing problem facing churches today. Hundreds of churches have been sued as a result of the sexual molestation of minors by church workers. Unfortunately, some church leaders ignore this concern and fail to implement a child sexual abuse prevention program. They think, "no child has ever been molested in our church, so why worry?" This attitude of denial is a very dangerous response to what one church insurance executive has called "an epidemic." Doing nothing to respond to this significant risk may subject a church to "punitive damages" (which ordinarily are not covered by a church's liability insurance policy) and can expose board members to personal liability. The lack of a prevention program leaves the children, the church, and church leaders vulnerable.

It Can Happen In Your Church

Incidents of molestation can occur in any church—*including yours*. Churches have traditionally accepted the services of anyone expressing an interest in working as a volunteer with children or youth. Churches are by nature trusting and unsuspecting institutions. Asking sensitive questions of those who are giving their time and talent can be seen as distasteful by church leaders. No one wants to offend potential workers, especially longtime church members with a history of good service. These qualities can make a church susceptible to incidents of child molestation.

Impact

A single incident of child molestation can devastate a church and divide the congregation. Members become outraged and bewildered; parents question whether their own children have been victimized; the viability of the church's youth and children's programs is jeopardized; and church leaders face blame and guilt for allowing the incident to happen. Such incidents often result in massive media attention, sometimes on a national scale. Television stations conduct live minicam broadcasts from church property on the evening news. Front page stories hit the local paper. Community residents begin to associate the church with the incident of molestation. But far more tragic is the emotional trauma to the victim and the victim's family, and the enormous potential legal liability the church faces. And if a trial ensues, the issue stays alive in the media for months, sometimes even years.

The Good News!

Church leaders can take relatively simple, yet effective, steps that significantly reduce the likelihood of child sexual abuse in your church. This book sounds an alert to the seriousness of this risk, but more importantly provides help so that your church can reduce the risk of such incidents from ever occurring. Now is the time to join thousands of other congregations that are taking positive steps to make their churches a safer place for children.

As you implement a preventive program, remember that the main objective is to provide a safe and secure environment for the children who are entrusted to your church. In seeking to accomplish this objective, you will be accomplishing another very important objective—reducing legal risk and liability exposure.

Now is the time to join thousands of other churches that are taking positive steps to make their churches a safer place for children.

2. Understanding Child Sexual Abuse

What Is Child Sexual Abuse?

The precise legal definition of child sexual abuse or molestation varies from state to state, but in general includes any form of sexual contact or exploitation in which a minor is being used for the sexual stimulation of the perpetrator. In a more common sense, child sexual abuse is:

> *"Any sexual activity with a child—whether in the home by a caretaker, in a day care situation, a foster/residential setting, or in any other setting, including on the street by a person unknown to the child. The abuser may be an adult, an adolescent, or another child, provided the child is four years older than the victim."* (National Resource Center on Child Sexual Abuse, 1992)

Child sexual abuse may be violent or non-violent. All child sexual abuse is an exploitation of a child's vulnerability and powerlessness in which the abuser is fully responsible for the actions.

Child sexual abuse is *criminal behavior* that involves children in sexual behaviors for which they are not personally, socially, and developmentally ready.

Child sexual abuse includes behaviors that involve touching and non-touching aspects.

Types of abuse that involve touching include:

- ❑ Fondling
- ❑ Oral, genital, and anal penetration
- ❑ Intercourse
- ❑ Forcible rape

13

Types of sexual abuse that do not involve touching include:

- [ ] Verbal comments
- [ ] Pornographic videos
- [ ] Obscene phone calls
- [ ] Exhibitionism
- [ ] Allowing children to witness sexual activity

The full extent of child sexual abuse in our country is not known. Current conservative estimates suggest that from 500,000 to over 1,500,00 children are sexually abused each year. The possibility that the number is higher is likely because the greatest percentage of these cases go unreported. The latest national retrospective study on the prevalence of child sexual abuse found that 27 percent of adult women and 16 percent of men claimed to have experienced some form of child sexual victimization. Over 25 percent indicated this occurred before the age of nine (Finkelhor, Hotaling, Lewis and Smith, 1990).

Child sexual abuse occurs in all demographic, racial, ethnic, socio-economic, and religious groups. Strangers account for less than 20 percent of the abusers. Estimates indicate that when a known assailant commits the abuse, half of the time it is a father or stepfather, and the rest of the time it is a trusted adult who misuses his or her authority over children.

The Effects of Child Sexual Abuse

"The personal violation of child sexual abuse causes the victim to experience many losses .... including loss of childhood memories, loss of healthy social contact, loss of the opportunity to learn, loss of bodily integrity, loss of identity and self-esteem, loss of trust, loss of sexual maturity, and loss of self-determination. All of these personal violations mean that victims of child sexual abuse lose the child's right to a normal childhood. In adulthood it may also mean the loss of the capacity to appreciate sexual intimacy as nurturing, holy, and loving." (The Report of the Winter Commission, 1990, Vol. 1, p. 118)

Child sexual abuse robs children of their childhood and can potentially scar its young victims for life. Too often in the past, the effects of abuse were minimized or dismissed. Children were viewed as being resilient. Recent research has shown that children can suffer significant pain from even a single abusive incident. Church members must be aware of the pain and long term suffering that can accompany such abuse. Abused children can display a wide range of negative symptoms in the aftermath of abuse. Abuse can result in abnormal fears, post traumatic stress disorder (PTSD), aggressive behavior, sexual "acting out," depression, diffused sexual identity, and poor self-esteem

(Kendall-Tackett, Williams, and Finkelhor, 1991). The incidence of sexually transmitted disease is also a possible outcome.

The degree of damage depends upon several factors including the intensity, duration, and frequency of the abuse. In addition, the *relationship* of the perpetrator to the child matters. If the abuser is a known and trusted authority figure in the child's life, the degree of impact increases dramatically.

> *An additional burden for the parishioner or client is a sense of being betrayed by God and the Church. This betrayal by one's pastor represents a major obstacle to the parishioner or client's personal faith. The damage to one's spiritual life done by this experience is often profound and long term* (Marie Marshall Fortune, *Sexual Violence: The Unmentionable Sin*, p. 107).

Consequences of child sexual abuse can plague victims into adulthood. Outcome studies of adult survivors of child sexual abuse suggest the following affects: sexual dysfunction, eating disorders, substance abuse, promiscuity, disassociation from emotions, and possible perpetration of sexual abuse on others (Geffner, 1992). When church leaders, pastors, and respected congregational workers perpetrate the abuse, lifelong religious confusion and deep feelings of enmity toward God and the church can occur.

The Profile of a Child Molester

> *Bob sat dejectedly before the church board. His broad shoulders slumped as he tearfully retold his story. Bob has been sexually molesting his thirteen year old daughter for the last two years. This activity may have gone undetected except that Bob tried to abuse one of his daughter's girlfriends while chaperoning a Sunday School activity. The young girl reported the incident to her parents and Bob was apprehended. The church leaders hearing this confession sat in disbelief. How could Bob, a successful businessman, husband, father of three children, and respected church worker commit such actions?*

Who is the typical child molester? Some church leaders assume that molesters are "strangers wearing trenchcoats" or "dirty old men." These stereotypes not only are inaccurate, but they dangerously contribute to a false sense of security. Researchers in the field of child sexual abuse currently indicate that no one profile fits the various perpetrators of abuse. Church leaders can become preoccupied screening stereotypes, while not suspecting the real molester could be an active adult or teen in the church. Consider the following:

❑ Over eighty percent of the time, the abuser is someone known to the victim

❑ Most abuse takes place within the context of an ongoing relationship

15

Symptoms of Molestation

Church workers and staff should be alert to the physical signs of abuse and molestation, as well as to behavioral and verbal signs that a victim may exhibit. Some of the more common signs are summarized below (Sloan, 1983).

Physical signs may include:

- ❏ lacerations and bruises

- ❏ nightmares

- ❏ irritation, pain, or injury to the genital area

- ❏ difficulty with urination

- ❏ discomfort when sitting

- ❏ torn or bloody underclothing

- ❏ venereal disease

Behavioral signs may include:

- ❏ anxiety when approaching church or nursery area

- ❏ nervous or hostile behavior toward adults

- ❏ sexual self-consciousness

- ❏ "acting out" of sexual behavior

- ❏ withdrawal from church activities and friends

Verbal signs may include the following statements:

- ❏ I don't like [a particular church worker]

- ❏ [A church worker] does things to me when we're alone

- ❏ I don't like to be alone with [a church worker]

- ❏ [A church worker] fooled around with me

❑ The usual offender is between the ages of 20-30 years

❑ 20 percent of sex offenders begin their activity before the age of 18

❑ Child abusers often are married and have children

If abuse occurs in your church, a respected member will most likely be the molester. Emphasis upon "stranger danger" will leave your church ill prepared. While it's uncomfortable even to consider this, the most likely assailants include Sunday School teachers, religious educators, nursery or preschool workers, teachers in a church-operated school, camp counselors, scout leaders, "concerned" adults who volunteer to transport children to church, and clergy. Trusted adults—male or female—can easily mislead children and most incidents of child sexual abuse take place in the context of an ongoing relationship between the abuser and the child.

*Most of the time,
the abuser is someone
known and trusted
by the victim.*

3. The Church's Legal Vulnerability

Why Churches Are Susceptible

Churches have unique features that can make them susceptible to incidents of child molestation.

Trust. Churches tend to be trusting and unsuspecting institutions. Even when questions are raised about a worker's conduct, church leaders may ignore the evidence rather than question the worker's character or motives.

Lack of Screening. Some churches do nothing to "screen" youth workers. Complete strangers may be accepted to work with children without any investigation whatever.

Opportunity. Churches provide ample opportunities for unsupervised close personal contact between adults and children. This risk increases dramatically for overnight activities.

Access. The Boy Scouts, Big Brothers, and similar organizations have instituted comprehensive programs to reduce the risk of child molestation. Child molesters are attracted to an institution in which they have immediate access to potential victims in an atmosphere of complete trust—*the church.*

Need. Most churches struggle to get adequate help for children and youth programs. Recruiting nursery workers, for example, can become an unending effort. Turnover among volunteer workers is also high. A willing volunteer worker provides welcome relief.

The Response of the Insurance Industry

No one evaluates risk better than insurance companies. Some companies are reducing the coverage they provide for child abuse or molestation, and in some cases are excluding it entirely. Most policies exclude damages based on intentional, criminal conduct (most acts of sexual molestation involve criminal activity). *Your church board should immediately review your church liability policy to determine whether you have any coverage for acts of molestation occurring on your property or during your activities, and if so, whether your coverage has been limited in any way.* Many churches will discover that they either have no coverage for such incidents, or that the policy limits have been significantly reduced. If you fit within either category, the procedures recommended in this book are of even greater relevance.

Why Litigation Is On The Increase

In the past, few victims of sexual molestation sued the perpetrator or the church. This reluctance has changed dramatically. The following factors provide a partial explanation of this new trend:

1. Media attention. The media has focused attention on child molestation cases, and especially on those cases involving church workers. Often, front page publicity is given to these cases, and to the astronomical jury verdicts that sometimes are awarded. The possibility of a huge verdict lures some victims into the courtroom.

2. Statute of limitations. Many states have greatly liberalized the period of time (the "statute of limitations") during which molestation victims must file a lawsuit. This has enabled victims to sue churches many years after an incident of molestation.

3. Theories of liability. Innovative theories of liability have been introduced by plaintiffs' attorneys that have assisted molestation victims in recovering money damages.

4. Injury. The extent of the psychological and emotional injury experienced by victims of sexual molestation has only recently been fully appreciated.

5. Number of victims. Recent studies suggest that the number of adults who were sexually molested or abused as children is staggering. Some studies suggest that as many as 27 percent of adult females and 16 percent of adult males were victims of molestation as minors.

6. Report requirements. All 50 states require certain individuals ("mandatory reporters") to report known or reasonably suspected incidents of child abuse to state officials. This has exposed many cases of child abuse, and made victims less willing to remain anonymous.

7. Support for litigation. An increasing number of attorneys and victim advocacy groups are encouraging sex abuse victims to utilize litigation as a means to secure justice and promote personal healing.

The Legal Environment

The number of lawsuits brought against churches as a result of child sexual abuse has risen substantially over the last decade. Various factors have been cited for this increase (see *Why Litigation Is On The Increase* on page 20). Below are a few examples of recent lawsuits brought against churches as a result of sexual molestation:

➾ A mother sued her church and its pastor, alleging that her 10-year-old daughter had been repeatedly raped and assaulted by a church employee. The mother alleged that when the employee was hired, the church should have known that he had recently been convicted of aggravated sexual assault on a young girl, that he was on probation for the offense, and that a condition of his probation was that he not be involved or associated with children. Despite these circumstances, the individual was hired and entrusted with duties that encouraged him to come freely into contact with children.

➾ A church was sued as a result of the sexual abuse of a 3-year-old child that occurred in a church nursery. A court concluded that the church could be responsible since it did not exercise a sufficiently high degree of care in selecting the volunteer worker who committed the abuse. In particular, the court emphasized that the church had not interviewed the volunteer regarding her own history of child abuse, and did not conduct any "background check."

➾ A volunteer Sunday School teacher began picking up a second grade boy each Sunday morning and evening allegedly for church services, and on Thursday evenings to participate in a church visitation program. This relationship continued for two years, during which time the teacher frequently molested the boy.

➾ A 6-year-old boy was sexually assaulted during Sunday School class. The boy attended a class of 45 first and second graders at a local church. During "story time," the boy became disruptive, and the teacher allowed a teenage volunteer worker to "take him back and color" in an unused room. The adult teacher did not check on the boy for the remainder of the Sunday School session. The male volunteer allegedly abused and raped the boy, and threatened to hurt or kill him if he "told anyone."

➾ A youth pastor sexually molested a 13-year-old boy. The boy then began molesting his sister, attempting to "act out" what the pastor had done to him. The church had hired the youth pastor though church leaders knew he had been guilty of child molestation in the past.

These sample cases illustrate the growing number of lawsuits directed at churches today. Since many out-of-court settlements occur, no one knows the full extent of the legal activity. Churches engaged in litigation can suffer devastating financial consequences. Substantial attorney fees and court costs occur. Jury awards have been in the millions of dollars. Punitive damages are possible. Out-of-court settlements often involve hundreds of thousands of dollars. Insurance may cover only a portion of the final total and some churches will have no coverage at all.

Why Churches And Church Leaders Are Sued

Most of the lawsuits filed against churches for acts of child molestation have alleged that the church was legally accountable either on the basis of *negligent hiring* or *negligent supervision.* Both theories of liability are pivotal issues. The term *negligence* generally refers to conduct that creates an unreasonable risk of foreseeable harm to others. It connotes carelessness, heedlessness, inattention, or inadvertence. Negligent hiring simply means that the church failed to act responsibly and with due care in the selection of workers (both volunteer and compensated) for positions involving the supervision or custody of minors. A church may exercise sufficient care in the hiring of an individual, but still be legally accountable for acts of molestation on the basis of negligent supervision. Negligent supervision means that a church did not exercise sufficient care in supervising a worker.

Churches need to understand the extent of their liability. Churches are not "guarantors" of the safety and well-being of children. They are not absolutely liable for every injury that occurs on their premises or in the course of their activities. Generally, they are responsible only for those injuries that result from their negligence. Victims of molestation who have sued a church often allege that the church was negligent in not adequately screening applicants or for not providing adequate supervision. As noted above, some churches are willing to use just about anyone who expresses an interest in working in a volunteer capacity with the youth in the church (*e.g.,* boys or girls programs, Sunday School, children's choir, nursery, teenagers, camp). Applicants for compensated positions may not be extensively screened or closely supervised.

Assume that an incident of abuse occurs at your church, and that the minister is asked to testify during the trial. The victim's lawyer asks, "What did you or your staff do to prevent this tragedy from occurring—what procedures did you utilize to check the molester's background and supervise his/her work with children?" What would your minister say? If the answer is "nothing," you can well imagine the jury's reaction. The only question in the jurors' minds at this point is the size of the verdict.

The victim's lawyer asks, "What did you or your staff do to prevent this tragedy from occurring?" If the answer is "nothing," you can well imagine the jury's reaction. The only question in the jurors' minds at this point is the size of the verdict.

Part Two

Policy Formulation

Developing Effective Policies For Your Prevention Program

4. *Establishing Policies and Procedures*

A Fourfold Strategy

Effectively communicating the information contained in Part One of this book may make church leaders and congregational members aware of vital issues and concerns related to sexual abuse. A commitment may exist to do something. That awareness and commitment must be turned into a workable plan. Policies and procedures must be established that provide safeguards against child sexual abuse. Four critical areas require attention:

- ❑ *worker selection*

- ❑ *worker supervision*

- ❑ *reporting obligations*

- ❑ *response to allegations*

The policies and procedures presented in the following chapters of Part Two are based on legal theory and practical experience. Many of them are being successfully used in churches to reduce the risk and liability of child sexual abuse. Some of these policies and procedures may work well in your church or organizational context. Others may need to be adapted to meet your needs. In all cases, your church's attorney should review the policies before they are implemented. Reporting obligations, for example, vary from one state to the next and you need specific knowledge of your state law.

Before You Read Further—
A Needs Assessment
Checklist

The following checklist can help you to conduct a quick needs assessment of your policy needs. Please take a moment and check each statement which is true for your church.

Statements left unchecked indicate a procedure or policy area in which your church or organization may be vulnerable to abuse or possible litigation if an incident occurs.

❏ We currently screen all paid employees, including clergy, who work with youth or children.

❏ We currently screen all volunteer workers for any position involving work with youth or children.

❏ We do a reference check on all paid employees working with youth or children.

❏ We train all of our staff who work with children or youth, both paid and volunteer, to understand the nature of child sexual abuse.

❏ We train all of our staff who work with children or youth, both paid and volunteer, how to carry out our policies to prevent sexual abuse.

❏ We take our policies to prevent sexual abuse seriously and see that they are enforced.

❏ Our workers understand state law concerning child abuse reporting obligations.

❏ We have a clearly defined reporting procedure for a suspected incident of abuse.

❏ We have a specific response strategy to use if an allegation of sexual abuse is made at our church.

❏ We have insurance coverage if a claim should occur.

❏ We are prepared to respond to media inquiries if an incident occurs.

5. Recruiting And Selecting Church Workers

First church announces a new policy—all volunteers who work with youth and children must immediately complete a screening form. No exceptions will be allowed. Suddenly a backlash occurs from some congregational members.

> *"What's going on here," complains Bill. "This is an invasion of privacy. What are they going to do next . . . put up metal detectors in front of the Sunday School classes? The church must be a place of trust."*

> *"I don't mind helping out in the church nursery once in a while," remarks Anne, "but I don't see how this is going to work. Sometimes people have to be called at the last minute."*

It's one thing to create a screening policy—but it's another thing to make it work. Every church has committed members like Bill and Anne who may express sincere reservations about screening. In formulating screening procedures, attention must be given to the full range of concerns that may surface as a result of the policy.

In this chapter we'll examine the basic components of an effective screening policy. Concerns, like those of Bill and Anne, will be addressed in Part Three of this book under the section dealing with training and implementation procedures.

All Workers Require Screening—Both Paid and Volunteer

To ensure adequate legal safeguards, every church must implement an effective screening program. The manner in which this is done and the screening forms used should be a matter of careful thought by the church. As an organization, the local church depends upon both *paid workers* and a large number of congregational *volunteers*. This presents a challenge to any screening procedure.

Paid Employees

Without doubt, all paid church employees—including clergy—should undergo a thorough screening process as a part of the job application procedure.

If your church recruits an employee who later molests a child, a key legal issue will be the steps your church took to screen that individual. Any screening form your church uses must ask direct questions that enable you to identify applicants that should not work with youth or children. To a large extent, actual court cases shape what questions must be asked.

Failure to screen paid employees that work with children places the church and its leaders in serious legal jeopardy. Today, no court will tolerate irresponsible attention to this need. Fortunately, churches across the nation increasingly recognize the seriousness of this concern. As a result, screening is now beginning to receive the attention it deserves.

Volunteer Workers

In addition to paid employees, most churches also depend upon a large number of volunteer workers. Some of these volunteers work numerous hours every week. Others serve only a few hours a year. The vast majority of church volunteers work in some capacity with youth and children. These volunteers must also be screened. *Churches face the same legal vulnerabilities using volunteer workers as they do using paid employees.*

Screening paid employees can be direct and straightforward. Screening volunteers, though, may present some obstacles. Volunteers are often hard to recruit in sufficient numbers and may balk at having to answer questions that appear distrustful of them and invasive of their private lives. Program leaders may hesitate to enforce measures that potentially cause people to decline to serve. Nevertheless, if a church is to lower its legal risk—and provide a safe place for children, youth, and workers—screening must be done.

An effective screening process must take into account the tension that exists between legal demands and practical reality. In light of this dilemma, this book illustrates the use of two screening procedures.

Primary Screening Procedures

⊃ *To be used with all applicants and church workers, full-time or part-time, compensated or volunteer, including clergy, according to the guidelines set forth below.*

The first procedure, which we will refer to as a "primary screening procedure" provides the church with the best potential to reduce legal risk. This procedure consists of the following components:

❑ an employment application

❏ a screening form (see Appendix 2)

❏ a personal interview

❏ reference checks (see Appendix 3)

❏ completion of a criminal records check authorization form—to be used when considered appropriate (see Appendix 2)

Each component of the procedure should be completed before the person begins work at the church. This includes both paid employees and volunteer workers. For churches who did not screen current staff members, these procedures should be completed retroactively.

Use A Screening Form

At a minimum, the screening form should ask for the following:

❏ the applicant's name (identity should be confirmed by a state driver's license or other photographic identification)

❏ address

❏ a full explanation of any prior criminal convictions for sexual abuse, molestation, or related crimes

❏ the area of youth work the applicant is interested in

❏ any training or education in youth-related work

❏ a description of church membership over the past five years

❏ a description of church volunteer work over the past five years

❏ a description of any youth work (at churches or any other organization) over the past five years

❏ the names and addresses of two references

A sample screening form is printed as Appendix 2, along with explanatory notes. The screening form is not a substitute for an employment application for church workers. Rather it is a supplement to it. The screening form found in this book can be modified so that it does not duplicate information requested on the employment application. *In all cases, the final form used should be reviewed by an attorney familiar with your state law.*

Conduct A Personal Interview

Individuals applying for higher risk positions (e.g., boys groups, scouting groups, camps, overnight or largely unsupervised activities involving either male or female children or adolescents) should be interviewed by a responsible staff member who has been trained to screen children and youth workers. Law enforcement personnel and local offices of state agencies responsible for investigating reports of child abuse often have materials that can be used to train the staff member who will conduct interviews. So do other youth organizations such as Big Brothers/Big Sisters, the Boy Scouts, Girl Scouts, Boys Clubs, Girls Clubs, and YMCA/YWCA. Employees of these agencies ordinarily are more than willing to assist a church representative in learning how to conduct a screening interview. These resources should be utilized.

Make A Record Of Contacts With References And Prior Churches

Having an individual complete a screening form *is in itself not enough to protect a church and its members.* Significant protection only occurs if the church takes additional steps.

Contact each reference listed on the application and make a written record of each contact. Show the date and method of the contact, the person making the contact as well as the person contacted, and a summary of the reference's remarks. Such forms, when completed, should be kept with an indivual's original application. A sample form that churches can use to make a record of contacts with references and other churches is reproduced as Appendix 3 at the end of this book.

Contact each church in which the applicant has indicated prior experience in working with children or youth. Place in the application file a written record of all of the information contained in the preceding paragraph. These procedures should be done with all children and youth workers.

Should religious conversion make a difference for a youth worker who has been guilty of child molestation in the past?

Occasionally, such persons freely admit to a prior incident, but insist that they have since had a conversion experience and that they now present no risk whatever. The safest course would be to encourage such an individual to work in the church, but in a position not involving access to children or youth. This is a reasonable accommodation of the individual's desire to serve his or her church. A church that permits such an individual to work with children or youth, on the basis of the professed religious conversion, will have a virtually indefensible position should another incident of molestation occur. The church's defense—that the molester claimed to have been converted—would likely be viewed with derision by a civil court. Churches that place a known child molester in a position involving access to children are taking an enormous risk.

Of course, contacting references listed on a screening form raises a couple of important issues that are illustrated by the following examples.

> *Example. Tom applies for a position as a volunteer worker with the youth group at Second Church. He is asked to complete a screening form. He notes on the form that he worked previously with the youth group at First Church. A staff member of Second Church calls First Church and asks if it would be appropriate to use Tom in youth work. Does First Church have any reservations about his suitability for working with minors? Unfortunately, First Church refuses to respond on the basis of "legal risk."*

This is an increasingly common response by both secular and religious organizations. There is a reluctance to share any information about former workers for fear of being sued. What should your church do if you receive such a response? *Document the refusal by the other church or reference to respond to your inquiry.* Ideally, ask the other church or reference to send you a letter confirming its refusal to provide you with any information concerning the suitability of the applicant to work with minors. This will be excellent evidence of "reasonable care" on your part. You did all you could to check with the other church or reference. If the other church or reference refuses to send you such a letter, then document its refusal in a written contact summary (see Appendix 3).

> *Example. Questions are raised at First Church about some inappropriate "touching" of children by Don, a volunteer children's worker. Don is questioned about the alleged behavior, he voluntarily resigns from his position and leaves the church. Don begins attending Second Church, and volunteers to work in a children's program. A staff member at Second Church calls First Church and asks if they know of any reason why Don should not be used in the children's program.*

Many church leaders find themselves in this dilemma. They want to share information that may protect children in other churches, but they do not want to be sued. Is there any way to resolve this dilemma? Consider two points.

Qualified privilege. Many states recognize a "qualified privilege" on the part of employers to share information about former employees with other employers. This ordinarily means that such statements cannot be the basis for defamation unless they are made with "malice." In this context, malice means either that the former employer knew that the statements made were false, or that statements were made with a reckless disregard as to their truth or falsity. In other words, so long as you have a reasonable basis for the statements you make about a former worker, your remarks will be protected in many states by a qualified privilege. A local attorney can advise you whether or not your state recognizes a qualified privilege under such circumstances.

Release form. In many states you will be able to share your legitimate concerns about a former worker without fear of legal liability if the worker signs an appropriate release form that consents to your evaluation and releases you from any legal liability for any injury or damages caused by the

Practical Screening Tips

Churches should keep the following considerations in mind when implementing a screening procedure:

⟿ **Confirm identity.** If an applicant is unknown to church leadership, you should confirm his or her identity by requiring photographic identification (such as a state driver's license). Child molesters often use pseudonyms.

⟿ **Screen all workers.** The screening procedure should apply to new applicants as well as current staff members. Obviously, churches need to use some common sense here. For example, if your Nursery Director is a 70-year-old woman with 25 years teaching experience in your church, you may decide that reference checks are unnecessary. The highest risks involve male workers in both children's and adolescent youth programs that involve unsupervised or overnight activities. Persons in this category should be carefully screened. Be sure to consider all workers who will have contact with minors. For example, a number of cases involve molestation of children by church custodians.

⟿ **Lower risk.** Think of the screening procedure in terms of risk reduction. A church is free to hire workers without any screening or evaluation whatever, but such a practice involves the highest degree of legal risk. On the other hand, a church that develops an extensive screening procedure and utilizes it for all current and future workers has the least risk.

⟿ **Use professional help.** The services of a local attorney should be solicited in drafting an appropriate screening form to ensure compliance with state law. It is also advisable that such forms be reviewed by the church's insurance company for its comments. It is also desirable to share them with a local office of your state agency that investigates reports of child abuse.

⟿ **Examine sample forms.** Consult the application forms used by the Boy Scouts, Big Brothers, and similar organizations. As a result of numerous lawsuits, these organizations have developed detailed and highly effective application forms. Review these forms, and use them as resources when preparing your own application. The local office of the state agency responsible for investigating reports of child abuse may have application forms for you to examine, and they often are willing to review the application forms that churches prepare.

⟿ **Fulfill legal requirements.** Be sure you are aware of any additional legal requirements that apply in your state. For example, a number of states have passed laws requiring church-operated child-care facilities to check with the state before hiring any applicant for employment to ensure that the applicant does not have a criminal record involving child abuse or molestation. Again, you will need to check with a local attorney for guidance.

⟿ **Maintain confidentiality.** The church must treat as strictly confidential all applications and records of contacts with churches or references. Such information should be marked "confidential," and access should be restricted to those few persons with a legitimate interest in the information.

remarks you share. Of course, this is a legal document that should be prepared by an attorney. Note that sample release language is incorporated into the applicant's statement at the end of the screening application (Appendix 2).

Secondary Screening Procedures

⊃ *To be used only with occasional volunteer workers according to the guidelines set forth below.*

Our strong recommendation is that the primary screening procedure be used for *all workers,* both compensated and volunteer. This is particularly true if your church insurance policy excludes or significantly limits coverage for sexual misconduct.

Some congregations may experience resistance or administrative problems implementing a primary screening procedure for occasional volunteer workers who serve *only a few hours every year.* For example, some church members may serve one or two hours a year as a nursery attendant and often are recruited at the last minute. When such circumstances arise, screening problems such as the following may surface:

❑ Some may view screening as a violation of personal privacy

❑ Some may feel screening breaks down trust within the church

❑ Some may contend that screening is impractical to carry out

❑ Some may argue that screening is ineffective

These concerns have no value in a court of law or to a child who is molested. Yet, in some churches they may represent true barriers to the screening of volunteer workers. If a church relies only upon a primary screening procedure that volunteer workers systematically ignore, the goals of lowering legal risk and protecting children, youth, and workers become impossible to achieve.

In many cases the biggest problem to screening is an administrative one. Last minute staffing changes, especially in church nurseries, can present a church problems in finding the volunteer help needed. The temptation is for the church to bypass the screening process in order to find immediate help. The goal must be to ensure that these occasional workers are properly screened.

An innovative strategy is needed that maintains the integrity of the screening process and promotes comprehensive compliance by occasional volunteer workers. A secondary screening procedure addresses this concern. Its primary use is for occasional workers in the church nursery.

To be effective, congregational members must embrace the goals of all church screening procedures. Volunteers must understand and accept the church's need to provide a safe place for children. The components of a secondary screening procedure are similar to those of a primary screening procedure. This process requires the same thoroughness of screening, including reference and background checks, as does the primary screening process. The difference lies in the implementation strategy and the target audience—*occasional volunteer workers who serve only a few hours each year.*

Secondary Screening Policies And Procedures

1. For Occasional Volunteers Only. Emphasis must be given that a secondary screening procedure is for use only with occasional volunteers. These are individuals who only serve a few hours each year. All paid and regular volunteer workers must use the primary screening procedure.

> *Example. First Church hires a woman to assist weekly with the infant's nursery on Sunday morning. As a church employee, the worker must follow a primary screening procedure. A secondary screening procedure should not be used with paid employees.*

> *Example. Same facts as the above example, but the worker is an unpaid church volunteer. As a "regular ongoing worker," whether paid or not, member or not, the worker must use a primary screening procedure.*

> *Example. Same facts as preceding example, but the worker is an unpaid church volunteer who only helps in the nursery a few times a year. A secondary screening procedure can be considered.*

2. For Church Members Only. A secondary screening procedure is for church members only. Nonmembers must use the primary screening procedure. This is a key point. *To be effective, a secondary screening procedure must be coordinated with the church's membership application and interview process.* At the point of membership the church should collect the following information:

- ☐ name

- ☐ address

- ☐ a description of church membership over the past five years

- ☐ a description of volunteer church work over the past five years

- ☐ the names and addresses of two references

3. Require References. Individuals who transfer their membership from another church should do so through a letter of transferal that indicates that they are members in good standing of their previous church. Individuals without any former church affiliation should list references on their membership application. Reference checks should be conducted prior to membership acceptance.

> *Example. Ralph and Pat request an application for membership to First Church. Formerly, they were members of First Church in a different city. The application requests a letter of transferal that indicates that they were members in good*

standing of their previous church.

Example. Same facts as above, but Ralph and Pat have never been members of a church before. The application requests the names of two references. The chairperson for the membership committee contacts the references on the application using the reference follow-up form found in Appendix 3 (while designed for employment references, the form can easily be adapted for membership references).

4. Conduct A Membership Orientation. The membership application and interview provide an initial screening process. A membership orientation class can be used to introduce the prevention plan. During the orientation, all church policies concerning sexual abuse prevention should be explained. *Each member should understand that a secondary screening procedure form, such as the one reproduced in Appendix 4, must be completed before any volunteer work can be done with youth or children.* Members can be given the form for review purposes at the orientation meeting. Later, if a church member is called upon for nursery duty or some other responsibility involving children or youth and is asked to complete the form, he or she will understand what is being asked and why it is being asked. No one will be surprised or caught off guard by the screening policy.

Example. The first Sunday of each month, First Church sponsors a new members orientation. At the orientation, new members learn about the history of the church, plus an overview of church programs and other useful information. Included in the presentation is a review of the church's policies on volunteer service with youth, children, and nursery care. A positive focus is given to the church's concern about providing a safe and secure environment for all family members and church workers.

5. Follow The "Six Month" Rule. Volunteers should only be permitted to work with youth or children after they have been members of the church for a period of time (*e.g.*, six months). Such a policy gives the church an additional opportunity to evaluate applicants and volunteers, and will help to repel persons seeking immediate access to children.

Example. Bill and Martha Berry recently began attending the church. The Berrys volunteer to help in the church nursery. Even though the church is in need of nursery workers, until the Berrys are members for a specific amount of time, no volunteer service with children or youth can occur.

6. Volunteers With Criminal Abuse Violations Not Accepted. Adults who have been convicted of or plead guilty to either child sexual or physical abuse should not work with children or youth in a volunteer capacity.

Example. Prior to his religious conversion, Sam was convicted of sexually abusing a minor. While in prison he became a Christian, and now is an active and supportive church member. Sam volunteers to work occasionally in the church nursery. Church policy does not permit Sam to serve. Rather, he is asked to volunteer in an area not involving the supervision of youth or children. While not wanting to diminish Sam's commitment and conversion, the church must also fulfill its legal and moral obligation to provide a safe place for its youth and children. If Sam were to molest a child while serving the church, the church would be in a virtually indefensible legal position.

7. Adult Survivors of Child Abuse Must Meet With A Pastor Before Working With Children Or Youth. This policy is inserted because of litigation suggesting that it is negligent for a church to hire children's workers without asking them if they were themselves victims of child abuse. Some courts have said that the statistical correlation between persons who abuse children and who were themselves abused as minors is so high that this kind of question must be asked. This policy attempts to respond to these legal developments, while at the same time preserving as much as possible the confidentiality of this kind of information. Persons who are adult survivors of abuse should not automatically be disqualified from further consideration. Rather, this information simply imposes on the church a higher duty of care. This duty can be discharged in most cases simply by running a criminal records check on the individual. If it comes back with no record of any child abuse or molestation, and if there is no other indication that the applicant poses a risk (from references or previous churches), then there is no reason why the person cannot be used. Admittedly, this is a controversial procedure, but it accurately reflects the current legal realities that all organizations, including churches, must face.

> *Example. Pam volunteers to work in the church nursery. Pam leaves the question on the screening form blank that asks whether she was a victim of abuse as a child. She does make a confidential appointment to discuss her situation with the senior minister. During that appointment, Pastor Brown expresses her appreciation for Pam, and for Pam's willingness and courage to discuss this painful part of her past. Pastor Brown explains to Pam the legal reasons why the church must ask potential workers if they are victims of abuse (see comment 5 on the explanatory notes to Appendix 2.) Pastor Brown and Pam discuss her motivation for working in the nursery and review her past history of youth work. Following the discussion Pastor Brown conducts a criminal records check to confirm that Pam has had no previous problems in children or youth work. No previous problems exist and Pam is invited to serve in the nursery.*

8. Obtain An Agreement To Follow Policies. Finally, the volunteer must complete a secondary screening procedure form (see Appendix 4), and sign it agreeing to follow church policies with respect to working with children or youth. A verbal confirmation should be obtained that the member understands the commitments agreed to under the provisions of the secondary screening procedure. The church should carefully store all signed forms in a locked file.

> *Example. Lori, a member of the church for six months, is recruited on a one-time basis to serve in the church nursery as an assistant helper for one hour. Carol, the nursery coordinator, contacts Lori and explains that all nursery assistants must complete a "nursery screening form" (a secondary screening form) prior to serving. Carol reviews the form with Lori and asks Lori if she has any questions*

Primary and Secondary Screening Procedures

Key Factors	Primary Screening	Secondary Screening
Who should use the procedure?	All church workers, paid and volunteer, who work with minors. No exceptions for paid church workers, including clergy, or workers who are not members of the church.	To be used only with volunteer church members, who have been members for a certain length of time (*e.g.* six months), and used only if a primary screening procedure is untenable. An example of appropriate use may be for a mother who is recruited to assist in the church's nursery for one hour a few times a year.
Application form required?	Yes, an employment application form must be completed.	Yes, a church membership application form must be completed.
Screening form required?	Yes, Primary Screening Form, see Appendix 2.	Yes, Secondary Screening Form, see Appendix 4.
Interview required?	Yes, as part of the application process.	Yes, regular membership interview and an oral review of the secondary screening form at the time of its completion.
Reference check required?	Yes, prior to selection, see Appendix 3.	Yes, at the time of membership.

about it or about working in the nursery. Lori indicates that she received instructions about the process at her membership orientation. Lori completes the form and returns it to Carol. Carol reviews the form and then confirms with Lori her schedule to help in the nursery.

When the church first commences a screening procedure for volunteer workers, those already active in volunteer service should also complete the screening process. If any current volunteer has a criminal conviction or has plead guilty to sexual or child abuse, that individual must be sensitively relieved of any duties in working with youth or children. Any individual who is an adult survivor of abuse should meet with the pastor before continuing as a volunteer for the reasons stated above.

As noted earlier, how this procedure is implemented is critical to its success. That concern will be addressed later in this book.

Screening And Criminal Records Checks

The sample screening form found in Appendix 2 contains an authorization for a criminal records check. While every paid worker should sign this authorization, this does not mean that the church should do a criminal records check on every worker. Rather, criminal records checks ordinarily should be viewed as a procedure that may be desirable if questions are raised about a particular applicant or worker. The form should be completed by every applicant (paid or volunteer) for any position involving the custody or supervision of minors. The application should also be completed by current employees and volunteer workers having custody or supervision over minors.

What if your local law enforcement agency refuses to perform a criminal records check?

In some communities, local law enforcement officials refuse to perform criminal records checks on church workers. When this happens, how should a church respond? Consider the following steps:

Check with other law enforcement agencies. The local police department may be unwilling to help you, but the sheriff or highway patrol may be willing to do so. Be sure to emphasize that you are seeking the information to provide a safe and secure environment for the children in your church.

Request written confirmation. Here is an important tip: If a local law enforcement agency refuses to assist you, *request a letter confirming its refusal*. Have them state something like this: "We are responding to your request to provide criminal records checks on persons who will be working with minors in your church. We understand that your purpose in making this request is to screen workers so that you can provide a safe environment for the children who are engaged in your programs and activities. We regret to inform you that we are unable to grant your request. We cannot assist you in making your church a safer place for children by conducting criminal records checks on workers." Such a letter would be very valuable evidence in the event your church is charged with negligent hiring of a child molester.

Check with members of your church who are involved in law enforcement. Do you have any law enforcement personnel in your church? Sometimes they can be helpful in conducting checks.

Contact your city council. Sometimes city council members can encourage the police to conduct criminal records checks, especially when they realize that the purpose is to provide a safe environment for children.

What kind of criminal records check should you request?

Most church leaders are unaware that there are several different types of criminal records checks. The two main types are "name checks" and "fingerprint checks." Criminal records checks vary widely in terms of the geographic area covered. In many cases, a criminal records check will only cover records within a particular state. The FBI will conduct a nationwide search, but only for government agencies. The fee for conducting a criminal records check also varies, depending on the type of search. In many states, a "name check" only requires the individual's name (including any aliases or maiden names), date of birth, and address. Some states require the individual's social security number. In any case, a law enforcement agency will not conduct a search without the consent of the individual. This ordinarily is provided in a written release. Obviously, the language of such releases varies from state to state. The screening form reproduced as Appendix 2 contains a "generic" criminal records search authorization for illustrative purposes. Be sure to substitute whatever form is required by your local law enforcement agency. One final point—information regarding criminal convictions should be treated as highly confidential information, and safeguards must be established to ensure that this information is disseminated to no more than one or two individuals who will be involved in the decision of whether or not to use the individual as a youth worker in the church.

What if you discover that an applicant for youth work was charged with child abuse or molestation but not convicted?

Many churches have learned that an applicant for youth work was charged with child abuse or molestation, but never convicted. Does the lack of a criminal conviction mean that a church is free to use the individual? This is a difficult question. At a minimum, church leaders should contact the prosecutor's office or the police and ask about the case. Mention that you are considering using the individual in a position in the church that will involve contact with minors. Often, a representative of the prosecutor's office, or a detective or other investigating officer, will respond to inquiries from the church concerning the facts of the case. Such input will be very significant in evaluating an applicant's suitability for working with minors. Remember, there are many reasons why a person may not be convicted of the crime of child abuse or molestation. Often, prosecuting attorneys are consumed with "major" crimes, and do not have the resources to devote to every case of child molestation. In other words, you cannot safely assume that a person who is charged but not convicted of child molestation poses no risk to your church. Further investigation is imperative in such cases.

What kinds of criminal convictions disqualify an individual for youth work in the church?

A criminal conviction for a sexual offense involving a minor would certainly disqualify an applicant. In the case of pedophilic behavior (molestation of a pre-adolescent child) such a conviction should disqualify an individual *no matter how long ago it occurred* (because of the virtual impossibility that such a condition can be "cured"). Other automatic disqualifiers would include incest, rape, assaults involving minors, murder, kidnapping, child pornography, sodomy, and the physical abuse of a minor. Other crimes would strongly indicate that a person should not be considered for work with minors in a church. Some crimes would not be automatic disqualifiers, because they would not necessarily suggest a risk of child abuse or molestation. Some property offenses would be included in this list, particularly if the offense occurred long ago and the individual has a long history of impeccable behavior.

In some cases criminal records checks are mandated by state law.

Several states require any child-care provider to obtain criminal records checks on its workers. In many states, churches that operate a child care program are covered by these laws. If your church operates a child care program, be sure to confirm whether or not your state has such a law. If it does, check to see if church child care facilities are covered.

Is Screening Too Burdensome?

If the use of screening procedures and reference forms seem overly burdensome, consider the following:

⇨ One insurance company executive has described as "an epidemic" the number of church lawsuits as a result of acts of sexual molestation.

⇨ Your church liability insurance policy may exclude or limit coverage for acts of child molestation. If so, you have a potentially enormous uninsured risk. Reducing this risk is worth whatever inconvenience might be generated in implementing a screening procedure. Just ask any member of a church in which such an incident has occurred.

⇨ The screening procedure is designed primarily to provide a safe and secure environment for the youth of your church. Unfortunately, some churches have become targets of child molesters because they provide immediate and direct access to children in a trusting and often unsupervised environment. In order to provide protection for the youth of your church against such persons, a screening procedure is imperative.

↪ The relatively minor inconvenience involved in establishing a screening procedure is a small price to pay for protecting the church from the negative consequences that often accompanies an incident of molestation.

↪ In some cases, church board members may be personally liable for acts of child molestation.

---

*Is screening important?
Ask any member of a
church in which an
incident of sexual abuse
has occurred.*

---

6. Supervising Church Workers

The Problem of Negligent Supervision

Robert and Beth were startled to discover blood on the underpants of their two year old son, Timothy, after arriving home from church. Robert immediately concluded that Timothy had been molested while in the nursery. He quickly drove back to the church and found Pastor Reynolds still visiting with some members. Pastor Reynolds was stunned by the allegation. Last year the church had implemented thorough screening procedures and policies to prevent sexual molestation. He and Robert contacted Sally who was in charge of the nursery that Sunday. Sally explained that the two adult rule was carefully followed and at no time was Timothy or any of the other children in the nursery ever left alone with one attendant. According to Sally, no abuse occurred. The allegation caused her great emotional distress. Later a medical examination revealed that Timothy's bleeding was caused by a skin problem. No molestation had occurred. Everyone was greatly relieved. Sally was thankful she had followed the two adult rule.

What if only one worker had been in the nursery that morning? What if the medical test was inconclusive? It's not hard to see that a charge of abuse can take on a life of its own. The resulting emotional environment becomes intense and painful.

Churches can use reasonable care in selecting workers, but still be liable for injuries sustained during church activities on the basis of *negligent supervision*. Negligent supervision refers to a failure to exercise reasonable care in the supervision of church workers and church activities. Churches have been sued on the basis of negligent supervision in a variety of contexts, including sexual molestation of minors. As noted before, churches are not "guarantors" of the safety and well-being of those persons who participate in their programs and activities. Generally, they are responsible only for those injuries that result from their negligence. A number of courts have rejected attempts by persons injured during church activities to sue the sponsoring church on the basis of negligent supervision. Churches can reduce the risk of negligent supervision in a variety of ways as described below.

Supervisory Policies and Procedures

Use A Team Approach—The Two Adult Rule

Consider adopting a "two-adult" rule. Such a rule says that two adult supervisors should be present during any church activity. Preferably one of these adults would be a parent of one of the participating children or youth, or at minimum, someone over 21 years of age. This rule reduces the risk of sexual molestation, and also reduces the risk of false accusations of molestation by individuals seeking a quick legal settlement.

> *Example. Fred, a college student and a volunteer worker with the church's high school youth group, announces he is available for transportation if any of the members need a ride to group activities. Anne, a seventeen year old high school senior asks Fred for a ride. This violates the two adult rule. Such an arrangement would not be permitted.*

> *Example. Stan, the youth pastor wants to meet with each member of the youth group to get to know them better. He requests that the church reimburse his expenses to take each student out for a Coke. The board approves the request, but instructs Stan that two students must be present at each meeting and that he should not meet with any student alone, unless the parental permission rule, described below, is followed.*

> *Example. Randy, an adult member of First Church, volunteers to pick up a 10-year-old boy on his way to church each week. The boy lives with his mother, who is delighted to have a "father figure" express an interest in her son. This arrangement presents not only a risk of molestation, but also of false charges. It should be discouraged, unless a second adult is present with Randy every time the boy is picked up.*

Obtain Parental Permission

What about situations where an adult has a legitimate reason to be alone with a child? Church staff or volunteer workers should obtain the consent of the child's parent or guardian before going out alone with that child, or spending time with the child in an unsupervised situation. Workers should also notify an appropriate church leader of such meetings in advance. Children should also have parental permission for involvement in church sponsored programs or activities.

> *Example. Recently, drugs were discovered in the possession of a fourteen-year-old male member of the youth group while he was at school. Stan, the youth pastor, offers to pick him up after school on Tuesday with the hope of providing the boy adult support. This conduct violates the parental permission rule. Stan must first gain permission from the student's parents before a private meeting can occur. He should also notify the senior pastor of his intentions in advance.*

> *Example. A female member of the youth group explains she has a problem she*

cannot share with her parents and wants to meet the youth pastor alone after school to discuss it. She insists that the youth pastor not tell her parents. This meeting violates the parental permission rule. The youth pastor can meet with the student if a second, preferably female, volunteer worker is present.

Example. Fred volunteers to serve as a driver for the junior high outing this Sunday afternoon. Fred will be driving his daughter plus three other members of the youth group. Fred calls each of the parents to make sure the parents have given their permission for the students to attend the event, and to make arrangements for their transportation. This meets the conditions of the policy.

Example. Same facts as above, but the Youth Coordinator contacts each of the parents and arranges the transportation for Fred. This meets the conditions of the policy.

Example. Same facts as preceding example but no one contacts any parent. This violates the policy.

Discuss Suspicious Behavior Immediately

Any inappropriate conduct or relationships between an adult volunteer worker and a member of the youth group or a child should be confronted immediately and investigated. Prompt warnings should be issued when appropriate, and the situation monitored very closely. The adult worker's services should be terminated immediately for continued violation of such warnings, or for a single violation of sufficient gravity. Church staff should note when a member of the youth group appears aloof or withdrawn, or exhibits a marked personality change. This may indicate a problem that deserves attention.

Some conduct just deserves an initial comment.

Example. The church youth group is having a picnic at a local lake. Following a volleyball game, one of the male chaperons begins to massage the shoulders of one of the female youth members. They are seated at a picnic table surrounded by other students. A second adult chaperon discretely pulls the first one aside and comments, "You probably weren't aware, but giving massages falls outside of proper volunteer conduct."

Other conduct requires reporting.

Example. Same facts as the preceding example, but the volunteer worker walks the student to an isolated location and massages her shoulders while laying down on the ground next to her. A second volunteer sees what is happening and immediately reports it to the adult in charge.

Example. A male youth volunteer is seen kissing a female member of the youth group. The action is immediately reported to the pastor.

Discuss Potential Criminal Sanctions With Youth Workers

Adults who work with children and adolescent youth should understand that sexual relationships with minors can lead to a felony conviction and imprisonment in a state penitentiary. The law views such misconduct very seriously, as it should. Church workers also should understand that the church insurance policy may not provide them with a legal defense of a sexual misconduct charge, or pay any portion of a jury verdict assessed against them on account of such conduct.

Install Windows On Classroom Doors

If feasible, consider installing windows on the doors to all classrooms or other areas used by minors. The windows should be made out of shatterproof glass. Alternatively, the doors to such classrooms should be left open during use so that persons passing by can observe inside. Sunday School superintendents or other church leaders also should make random visits to all classrooms and frequently visit or inspect areas of church buildings that are isolated from view.

Provide Adequate Personnel

Programs that involve children and youth should always include adequate supervisory personnel. Supervision should also be maintained before and after the event until all children are in the custody of their parents or legal guardians.

> *Example. The elementary grade Sunday School classes frequently dismiss before the adult classes. While the parents remain in class, the children often run freely around church property. One Sunday, two ten-year-old boys sexually molest an unsupervised eight-year-old girl in a vacant classroom.*

> *Example. First Church has a rotating "Sunday Helper" volunteer who reports to the Sunday School Superintendent and fills in as an adult helper wherever needed for that morning. This worker assists in tasks such as supervising children or monitoring church facilities. Such a helper reduces the problem of inadequate supervision.*

Observe An Overnight Rule

Special attention must be given to overnight activities that involve youth. All adult chaperons and supervisors should be cleared in advance with the proper church leaders.

> *Example. Johnny is attending an overnight campout of his church's scouting program. At the last moment, his uncle who is visiting from another state volunteers to serve as an adult chaperon. Based on the overnight rule policy, plus the church membership policy, he does not qualify for an adult leadership role.*

Use A Church Nursery Identification Procedure

Procedures should exist for the church nursery that clearly identify the child and the child's parent or guardian. Children should only be released to a properly identified and preauthorized adult.

Example. First Church uses a "claim-check" system in its nursery. Adults sign their children in at the nursery and are given a plastic identification number that is also pinned to the child. The child can only be picked-up when the "claim-check number" is presented. The numbers are randomly assigned each week.

Example. Second Church keeps a Bulletin Board in its nursery of photographs of all the parents and children who use the nursery. Whenever a new family arrives, they get their picture taken. Nursery attendants release the child only to the adults in the picture. The photos are updated periodically, or whenever a change occurs in a child's legal guardian.

Adopt An Appropriate Children/Youth Worker's Policy Statement

Adopt in writing, a policy statement that articulates each separate policy such as those illustrated above. At a minimum, the policy should contain the following elements:

❑ A description of the selection process and qualifications for youth group leaders. Persons who are known to have committed previous acts of sexual misconduct should be strictly prohibited from serving. A screening procedure should be described. This is also where the "6-month rule" should be discussed.

❑ A complete definition of child sexual abuse.

❑ Behavioral parameters for all workers. Those kinds of relationships and contacts that are strictly prohibited should be specified, along with the consequences for violating these rules. Adult volunteers should be strictly prohibited from having sole custody of a member of the youth group with few exceptions (e.g., a younger brother or sister of the adult volunteer, or parental permission has been obtained and a member of the church staff has been notified in advance of the meeting).

❑ A description of those who are legally obligated to report reasonably suspected cases of abuse under state law. The policy should also mandate all church employees and workers to report any suspected cases of abuse to their program supervisor. (See Chapter 7). This will not necessarily relieve such persons of their legal duty to report suspected cases of abuse to the state.

❑ A list of other policies or procedures the church expects all workers to obey.

An attorney should review the policy statement.

A charge of abuse can take on a life of its own. The resulting emotional environment becomes intense and painful.

The Risk Meter

Legal Risk

How much legal risk does your church want to assume?

A church's response to the recommendations made in this book can be illustrated using a "risk meter" like the one above. On one side there is *low* risk and on the other side there is *high* risk. Where do you want the "needle" to register—near the *low* rating or the *high* rating? Each church will decide for itself where the needle will appear. For example, a church leader asks if the church can use someone who has been accused of abuse but who denies any wrongdoing. Or, a church would like to use a screening procedure that does not involve reference checks. What about not using a two-adult rule in the nursery due to a lack of helpers on a particular Sunday, or using a secondary screening procedure for workers who are not occasional volunteers or who are not church members? What about taking a father along on an overnight activity who shows up at the last minute and volunteers to help? Such questions come down to the issue of risk. How much legal risk does a church want to assume? Churches are free to use only one attendant in the nursery, or to conduct little if any screening of workers. These activities are not "illegal." But, the effect of this will be to move your needle over toward the *high* side of the meter. Keep the idea of a "risk meter" in mind as your church makes the many decisions that go into the implementation of a screening procedure. Remember, your decisions in creating and implementing a prevention program will determine where the needle will be on your "risk meter."

7. Reporting Procedures For Church Workers

Developing and following a reporting procedure is a critical component in a sexual abuse prevention program. Child sexual abuse thrives when it goes unnoticed or unreported. Often, an abusive situation continues because of someone's failure to report it. All church workers need to know what constitutes an occasion for reporting, the reporting channels they should use, and their obligations to make a report.

Reporting Obligations

An effective reporting procedure enhances the effort to protect children. Ordinarily, child molesters will not remain in a church where workers are trained to identify symptoms of child abuse and are encouraged to report suspicious behavior. Child abusers thrive on secrecy and are more likely to commit criminal acts in organizations where they go unnoticed.

State Compliance—A Legal Obligation

Church workers should be aware of state laws that govern the reporting of child abuse. Every state has a mandatory reporting law which specifies the following:

- ❏ What constitutes child abuse.

- ❏ Those persons ("mandatory reporters") who are legally responsible for reporting known and reasonably suspected cases of abuse. Most states require a direct report to a state agency.

- ❏ The length of time required to make a report. In most states, those providing professional care or services to children have a 48 hour period to make a report. In some states, an oral report is due within 24 hours.

- ❏ The nature and content of the report. Many states permit the reporter to remain anonymous. However, if an individual desires to remain anonymous, the report should be made over the phone in the presence of an attorney or other independent witness who can verify later, if necessary, the identity of the reporter. This may become important if the reporter later is charged with negligence for failing to make a report. If no witnesses to the report exist, and the report is done anonymously, providing a defense becomes problematic.

☐ The social agencies or department to be contacted. In some states, reports can be made to law enforcement officers.

☐ The criminal penalties for failing to report. Failure to report may be punishable by a fine or jail sentence.

☐ Protection from legal and civil litigation if the report is made in good faith.

Mutual Accountability—A Church Obligation

A sound reporting procedure promotes accountability among church workers. Questionable or inappropriate behavior often precedes acts of child molestation. Church workers should be trained to identify inappropriate behavior with children. Workers should be encouraged to warn each other when questionable behavior is displayed. Questionable behaviors should be reported to the proper individuals. Such a policy, if implemented with care and sensitivity, can help to avoid actual instances of abuse or molestation.

Personal Responsibility—A Moral Obligation

Workers may not report a suspected incidence of child sexual abuse for a variety of reasons. Some may want to avoid embarrassing situations. Who wants to be a tattle tale? A fear of possible personal and legal recrimination may exist. Discrete and confidential reporting of suspected abuse is critical to abuse prevention. Church workers should understand that reporting reflects caring and is not an act of disloyalty.

Developing A Church Reporting Procedure

A reporting policy should provide clear instructions to church workers concerning *when* a report should occur and *how* it should be made. Your policy should include the following:

☐ A clear rationale which explains the need for proper reporting and the obligation of workers to follow these procedures.

☐ The basis for making a report (e.g., policy violations—see Chapter 6).

☐ A description of possible indicators and symptoms of child sexual abuse. (See Chapter 2.) Workers should report to their supervisor when a child displays these indicators. Although they do not prove abuse, they are warning signs of possible problems.

☐ A procedure to follow when possible abusive or unhealthy activities are suspected. All reports should be documented in writing and brought immediately to the attention of your church's leadership.

Establish A Line Of Reporting

Church leaders should institute a line of reporting that should be followed in every case of suspected abuse. Reports of possible child abuse should be quickly communicated to the proper church leader. Reports reflect a serious obligation at the highest levels of church leadership. No report should be lost in "middle management."

> *Example. A leader in the church's scouting program confesses to the Youth Director that he has molested a 15-year-old boy in the program. He pledges it will never happen again. The Youth Director keeps the confession to himself. The Youth Director's actions violate the reporting policy guidelines. Under state law, the Youth Director may have a legal obligation to report the confession. A church reporting policy should mandate that any allegation be reported to the senior pastor.*

> *Example. A teacher in the preschool program notices a two year old girl has severe bruises on her legs and buttocks. She immediately reports the information to the Preschool Director. The Director reports the information to the Senior Pastor and also reports to the county office of Youth and Family Services.*

➲ ***Important: In many states both compensated and volunteer church youth workers will be mandatory reporters. Do not assume that requiring such persons to report suspected abuse to a designated church official will discharge their reporting duty under state law. These workers may still have a duty to report the suspected abuse to the state. State law must be consulted.***

Reporting To The State

> *Example. A 4th grade Sunday School teacher asks her class members to write down prayer requests on individual pieces of paper. One girl writes "I want my daddy to stop hurting me." The teacher is shocked by this statement, and immediately shares it with the pastor who advises her to question the girl about the statement after class on the following Sunday. The teacher does question the girl, who becomes defensive and insists that she was merely attempting to have the most dramatic prayer request.*

> *Example. A mother and her 4-year-old daughter stop by the church office while the pastor is present. They all spend several minutes in conversation. At one point, the girl makes a statement strongly indicating that she is being abused by her step-father. The mother quickly takes the girl to a back room and questions her. A few minutes later they emerge, and the mother insists that the child was "fantasizing."*

> *Example. A teenage girl informs her youth pastor that her father has been sexually*

molesting her. The youth pastor immediately informs the senior pastor, who confronts the father with the allegation. The father (a respected member of the church) vigorously denies the charge.

Is there a legal duty to report any of these incidents to the state? These cases illustrate the difficulty that church staff encounter in making this important decision. Here are some factors to consider in deciding whether or not to report a particular incident of suspected abuse to the state:

(1) *Are you a mandatory or merely a permissive reporter under state law?* Mandatory reporters (as defined by state law) face criminal penalties for not reporting. Permissive reporters are permitted to report but they are not legally required to do so. However, it is possible that permissive reporters who do not report reasonable suspicions of abuse will be sued later by victims who allege that their suffering was perpetuated by the failure to report. Therefore, do not automatically dismiss a duty to report on the ground that you are merely a permissive reporter under state law.

(2) *What is the definition of child abuse in my state?* Surprisingly, some states define abuse very narrowly to include only abuse inflicted by a parent or caretaker.

(3) *Do I have reasonable cause to believe that abuse has occurred?* Remember, most state laws require mandatory reporters to report not only actual abuse, but also reasonable suspicions of abuse. Our recommendation—interpret "reasonable cause" very broadly. Also, note that child abusers, when confronted with their misconduct, often deny it. Any allegation must be treated seriously.

(4) *Be especially aggressive when dealing with pedophilic behavior* (that is, sexual molestation of a pre-adolescent child). Some studies suggest that a pedophile may have hundreds of victims over the course of a lifetime. You have a duty to protect other innocent victims. Resolve doubts in favor of reporting.

(5) *Be especially aggressive when dealing with suspected abuse on the part of a person with a history of previous abusive behavior.* Resolve doubts in favor of reporting.

(6) *Does the clergy-penitent privilege apply?* In a few states, clergy who learn of child abuse during a confidential counseling session are not required to report the information to the state.

(7) *Consider discussing the case anonymously with a representative of the state agency that receives reports of abuse.* These representatives often are more than willing to discuss particular cases and evaluate whether or not a report should be filed. Of course, if you are advised that a report need not be filed, be sure to obtain the representative's name and make a record of the call.

(8) *Consider filing an anonymous report from the office of some independent third party* (such as a local attorney or the pastor of another church). The other person can later verify that you in fact made the report.

(9) *If you have any doubts concerning your duty to report an particular incident to the state, an*

attorney should be consulted. It is also desirable to inform your insurance agent.

Train Workers And Volunteers.

Conduct periodic training of workers and staff regarding the reporting procedures. This is especially important at the beginning of a new program schedule or whenever a new person begins working in a ministry or program. Training sessions should present the church's policy on reporting and the rationale behind it. Workers should have the opportunity to voice their concerns and questions. All church staff should know their obligation to report a possible incident, and the necessity to provide feedback to one another concerning questionable behavior. The church does not want to create an atmosphere of fear or suspicion. Proper training can help workers see how reporting and personal reminders can be done honestly and discretely without generating undue suspicion or anxiety.

⊃ **Tip:** *Be sure to check your state child abuse reporting law regularly. State legislatures tend to amend these laws often. Church leaders need to be aware of any changes.*

Child sexual abuse thrives when it goes unnoticed or unreported.

8. Responding To Allegations Of Abuse

Be Prepared In Advance

This book has emphasized the necessity of prevention. Realistically no practical prevention strategy is 100 percent effective. An accusation of child sexual abuse may occur in any church. Churches need to develop a premeditated plan or strategy to respond to sexual abuse allegations. Your church should not try to navigate a crisis situation without a compass to guide you. Wrong reactions can multiply the pain and liability inherent in an abuse case. An effective response strategy recognizes the following underlying principles:

❑ All allegations need to be taken seriously.

❑ Situations must be handled forthrightly with due respect for people's privacy and confidentiality.

❑ Immediately contact your insurance carrier.

❑ Full cooperation must be given to civil authorities under the guidance of your church attorney.

❑ Adequate care must be shown for the well-being of victims.

❑ The victim should not be held responsible in anyway.

Creating a Response Plan

In light of the above principles, a thorough response plan should be developed. If possible it should be reviewed with your church's attorney and insurance agent. The following factors should be kept in mind.

Maintain Adequate Records

Always have adequate records of workers' applications, references, and screening forms. They should be up-to-date and accessible.

Select A Spokesperson

Designate a specific spokesperson for your church. This person should be able to speak to the media and the congregation regarding the matter in a discrete, informed, and diplomatic way. In some cases, the media interviews several church leaders who have never given any consideration to responding to such inquiries. In such cases, conflicting and contradictory statements can abound, and the public will develop a negative impression of the church. This is avoided if only one person is designated to speak for the church in such cases.

Know Your Reporting Obligations

Know your state's reporting requirements. States differ in terms of behaviors that should be reported and which persons are mandated to report suspected abuse. This information is available from your local Department of Youth and Family Services, district attorney's office, or local law enforcement agencies. In addition, determine which local agencies are responsible for investigating possible abuse.

Use A Reporting Procedure

Develop a clear reporting procedure for all programs that work with youth or children. Workers should be instructed as to what behaviors should be reported and to whom they should report. Workers should be assured that state law protects them from liability when they report actual or suspected abuse, so long as they do not act maliciously.

Prepare A Position Statement

Develop for public use a clear position statement of your church regarding child sexual abuse. Include your policies and established safeguards. This statement can be released if an allegation of abuse occurs. Having a carefully prepared statement is far superior to making no comment. This is your opportunity to influence public opinion positively by emphasizing your awareness of the problem of child abuse, your concern for victims, and the extensive steps your church has taken to reduce the risk and provide a safe environment for children. Show the media this book, and the accompanying audio and video tapes. Let them know that you take this risk seriously, and that you have acted responsibly. Describe all the precautions you have taken, and the policies you have implemented. This is no time for silence or "no comment." Do not surrender the bully pulpit to those who will criticize and condemn you.

Don't Engage In Denial, Minimization, Or Blame

Many churches, when confronted with an allegation of abuse, respond in one or more of the following ways: (1) Deny that the incident occurred, despite clear evidence to the contrary. (2) Acknowledge that the incident occurred, but minimize it. For example, a church leader may say, "it only happened once," or "it wasn't that serious." (3) Blame the victim or the victim's family. These responses are all inappropriate and should be avoided.

Use An Attorney

Always have your attorney present while answering any investigative questions from the police or social service agencies.

Don't Be Accusatory

Avoid spelling out the details of an accusation in a public interview.

Work With Your Denomination And Insurance Company

Work closely with your insurance company. If your church is a part of a larger faith group or denomination, contact your group's governing organization and obtain information about specific guidelines and procedures that they endorse.

If An Allegation Occurs

In the case of an actual allegation follow these guidelines:

1. Document all your efforts at handling the incident.

2. Report the incident immediately to your church insurance company, attorney, and denominational officials. Do not try to handle this without professional outside assistance.

3. Contact the proper civil authorities following the guidance of your insurance company and attorney. Do not attempt an in-depth investigation. This should left to professionals who are familiar with these cases.

4. Notify the parents.

5. Do not confront the accused until the safety of the child or youth member is secured.

6. Do not prejudge the situation., but take the allegations seriously and reach out to the victim and the victim's family. Showing care and support help to prevent further hurt. Extend whatever pastoral resources are needed. Remember that the care and safety of the victim is the first priority. In some situations, churches have responded in a negative or nonsupportive manner to the alleged victim. This can increase the anger and pain of the victim and the victim's family. Future reconciliation will be more difficult and the possibility of damaging litigation increases.

7. Treat the accused with dignity and support. If the accused is a church worker, that person should be relieved temporarily of his or her duties until the investigation is finished. If the person is a paid employee, arrangements should be made to either maintain or suspend his or her income until the allegations are cleared or substantiated.

8. Use the text of the prepared public statement to answer the press and to convey news to the congregation. Be careful to safeguard the privacy and confidentiality of all involved.

An accusation of child sexual abuse may occur in any church. Wrong reactions can multiply the pain and liability inherent in an abuse case.

Part Three

Training and Implementation Procedures

9. Safeguarding The Church Through Training And Education

Barb and Tom both teach in the church's elementary education program on Sunday mornings. Today they received a memo from Pastor Green mailed to all teachers announcing that the church was adopting new policies to protect children from sexual abuse. All Sunday School teachers had to complete the enclosed screening form and return it to the church office. Tom was a bit puzzled.

"This is the first I've heard of this. Have you heard anything?"

"No," replied Barb. "I wonder if some problem has occurred."

"I don't know, but the questions on this form are very personal. You'd think there would be some explanation about this whole thing before we got a form like this in the mail."

Developing an Educational Strategy

Introducing policies such as those proposed in Part Two requires careful thought and preparation. Church members and volunteer workers should be prepared in advance before actual implementation procedures begin. Using an appropriate educational strategy to inform congregational members and train church workers can make the difference between a successful or a failed prevention program.

A comprehensive educational strategy provides the foundation for your prevention program. Instruction concerning child sexual abuse and the purpose of the prevention program comprise a critical part of the curriculum. The training of workers makes up the balance of the curriculum. To be effective, an educational effort needs to be intentional, systematic, and sustained.

Intentional instruction involves a clear sense of what you are trying to achieve. Your instructional effort should have a clear statement of goals that provides a powerful rationale for the prevention program.

Systematic instruction targets the entire congregation. Specific instruction should be provided to church leaders, program directors, volunteers, and to the congregation as a whole.

Sustained instruction recognizes that a "one shot" approach will not work. Workers and leaders change frequently in churches. Child sexual abuse training must be included as a part of the church's yearly curriculum.

Target Audiences And Training Strategies

Let's examine how an educational strategy applies to the various audiences related to church life.

Leadership

Church leaders require extensive teaching and training on this issue. Training should be done to impart both vision and commitment. First, leaders must understand the potential danger of child sexual abuse and why churches must do something to prevent it from occurring. Second, leaders must develop a commitment to implement a prevention plan. Third, leaders need to understand the legal basis for policy decisions and the rationale for changes that may be required to implement a plan. In essence, leaders require education and training regarding the entire contents of this book. Furthermore, that training must continue over time. As new leaders enter service, they will require an orientation to this issue. In addition, leaders must stay informed regarding changes in the law that affect the church's program. This is now possible through the *Church Law & Tax Report Informational Support Program* (see Appendix 7).

This book, the *Church Leader Alert* training tape (audio cassette) on "Sexual Molestation and the Church," and the video training tape that are part of our sexual abuse prevention resources provide an excellent starting point in leadership training and education. (See Appendix 7 for a complete description of these and other resources). The audio cassette tape allows church leaders to quickly become informed. They can listen to the tape as they drive to work. The video tape should be shown and discussed at a board meeting or leadership retreat using the leader's guide that comes with the video.

The Family

The family remains the most critical and necessary place for prevention education to occur. The church should make available to parents information about child sexual abuse. The first segment of our video tape can be used in conjunction with adult Sunday School classes or special workshops to help educate parents concerning child sexual abuse and why the church is implementing a prevention program.

Parents are to be encouraged to instruct their children about the nature of abuse. Recent research indicates that over 94 percent of parents wish to be a part of their child's education in this area (Wurtele, Kvaternick, and Franklin, 1992). Parents are often reluctant to teach their children that

64

they can be victimized by people they know. The church should work closely with parents to provide balanced materials and techniques for home instruction. In addition, the church should provide education through its youth programming to instruct teens about the dangers of sexual abuse.

Church Workers

A prerequisite to establishing a solid prevention program requires regular in-service training of all workers involved with children and youth. Due to the frequent changes in church staff and volunteers workers, continual training must be built into all programs that work with youth and children. Our video can be used for staff training. Ideally such training should occur in a group setting, but when the need arises individuals can view the tape at home. The church can obtain literature from various state and community agencies that handle abuse cases. Social workers from your local Department of Social Services can speak to your staff. Workers especially need to know the following:

- ❑ The definition of child abuse

- ❑ Sexual and physical abuse symptoms

- ❑ What constitutes inappropriate conduct

- ❑ Church policies that govern working with children or youth

- ❑ The civil and criminal consequences of misconduct

- ❑ Reporting procedures for observed or suspected misconduct

- ❑ The rationale behind screening procedures

The Congregation

Church leaders should accept the responsibility to educate congregational members concerning the problem of sexual abuse in our society, and why the church is developing a sexual abuse prevention plan. Sermons, bulletin inserts, letters, newsletter articles, and special adult Sunday School classes are just a few of the mediums available to achieve this goal. A new members orientation class should be used to explain church policies and procedures to all individuals who join the church.

Adult Survivors of Sexual Abuse

Your church probably has members who are adult survivors of child or adolescent sexual abuse. Your attention to this topic will stir up painful memories and feelings for these individuals. You may even have adults who are active molesters. As you address this topic be prepared to respond to the needs of these individuals with care and support. Adult survivors of abuse need both information and support. Adult survivors will benefit from a community of acceptance and concern. Support groups provide a powerful source of healing. Consider starting such a group, perhaps through your local ministerial association. A crucial concern is to find capable leaders who have professional training to address the issues that will be involved. Consult with your local Department of Youth and Family Services to determine what resources are available in your community.

The Public

The media has capitalized on the sensational nature of sexual abuse within the church. While it is true that the church faces a problem in this area, the same can be said for all institutions involving children and youth. What is not as commonly known is the concern and attention that church leaders from almost every denomination are giving to this issue. The church must proactively address this issue and let the public know of its commitment to safeguard children. Press conferences, community workshops, letters to the editor, and appearances on local television and radio programs provide ways for the church to generate public awareness of the problem *and* the solution. Your church's policy regarding child sexual abuse should be shared with representatives of the police department and your local family service agency. Denominational officials should develop and promulgate a position paper on this topic. An excellent example of this has been provided by the Catholic Archdiocese of Cincinnati's *Decree on Child Abuse*. A sample press release from a local ministerial association is included as Appendix 5.

Expect An Emotional Response

Discussing a preventive program for child sexual abuse in your church will trigger a variety of emotional reactions. As with any program that requires change and involves an element of discomfort, you should expect both support and resistance. For many, trust is at the heart of the church. Screening procedures may be viewed as violating that trust. Some people will experience deep emotions because of their own past experiences with abuse. Leaders and workers may have legitimate concerns regarding the nature of policies and the consequences to their ministries if these policies are implemented.

To help in overcoming congregational resistance, church leaders need to anticipate concerns and reduce fears regarding this controversial issue. Effective education and training requires an implementation strategy. The following chapter describes such a plan.

10. Implementation Procedures

Establishing An Effective Prevention Program

This book is designed not only to inform but to motivate churches and other volunteer organizations to begin child sexual abuse prevention programs. Prevention programs reduce both the risk of child sexual abuse and the legal liability of the church and its leaders. To work, however, policies and procedures, and training and education, must be effectively implemented. This chapter illustrates an implementation strategy.

How You Can Change Your Church

Initial attempts to change your church may result in frustration. People resist change for a number of reasons. Some people are happy with the status quo while others will react emotionally to the topic of child sexual abuse. Certain members of your church will resist policy changes that do not solicit and include their input. Others will balk at the extra time and inconvenience new policies may require. Implementing a prevention program requires a strategy that considers the dynamics and ethos of your church. No one blueprint will work for every congregation.

Levels of Influence

Picture your church as three concentric circles. In the center are the people with the most influence, usually clergy and formally recognized leaders. Every church also has opinion leaders who have a lot of informal power, even though they may or may not hold a specific office. These leaders may reflect 5 to 10 percent of the congregation's membership, but they account for 90 percent of the ideas that guide the church. Gaining the support of level one leaders is critical in order to launch a prevention program. In a hierarchial church, where policy flows from the top down, one individual may legitimize a program. In a congregational church, where power arises from within the membership, the support of key opinion leaders is vital. Proposing a rationale for the program is insufficient to gain support. Proponents must anticipate concerns, and be able to reduce the fears of these key leaders. Otherwise the program is dead in the water. While the support of these leaders is necessary to launch the program, it is insufficient to make it work. Let's move to the second and third circles.

The second circle represents church employees, ministry leaders, and volunteer workers. They carry out the main ministries of the church. For any policy to be effective, these individuals must see that it is carried out. Without their support and commitment, the policy will be no more than empty words. These people must be enlisted to support the effort, considered in policy formation, and educated and trained to implement and enact the policies and procedures. In essence, if they are to conduct the mission, they must share the vision.

ministry leaders

church leaders

volunteer workers, employees

congregational members

The third circle represents the congregation-at-large: those who primarily attend and participate. These individuals should understand the policies and their support should be solicited. Church unity requires that all policy decisions be implemented in a way that considers the needs of congregational members. Communication is vital to achieve this goal.

With these factors in mind, let's consider how one strategy might unfold.

An Implementation Strategy

The following steps present a sample model of an implementation process. Your church is unique and will require some modifications to the following plan. Nevertheless, you should be able to adapt it to meet your needs.

1. Find your leader. Ideally, a successful prevention program begins with people who deeply care about the issue of child sexual abuse. You may be one of those people. Others may include a staff member, business administrator, board member, Sunday School teacher, or a person who has experienced the pain of abuse. Form a task force that can make a presentation to your church leaders. Find one person to serve as the leader. What if your church has no one who deeply cares about this issue? You must still proceed out of moral and legal necessity. Organize several people to serve as a task force. Guidance can come from this book and other available resources to reduce sexual molestation in the church.

2. Obtain the support of key church leaders. Your task force should make a presentation to your governing board. At this point, the goal is not to present a detailed prevention plan, but only to gain support for the concept. Focusing on details now will lead to problems. Attention should be given to the following points:

- ❏ Child sexual abuse can happen in your church

- ❏ One incident can devastate a child, a family, and the church

- ❏ The legal liabilities can be enormous

- ❏ Church leaders may be held liable

- ❏ A prevention program can reduce risk through relatively simple procedures

Use the materials in Part One of this book to prepare the presentation. Be prepared to respond to the following concerns:

❏ *The risk of this happening in our church is small*

> **Response.** The *Los Angeles Times* has called this *the worst problem facing the church in centuries* (May 17, 1992). Focus on the legal and moral obligations of the church. Are those leaders raising this concern willing to assume the legal risks if an incident should occur? If an incident occurs, issues of negligent selection and negligent supervision will focus directly upon the actions and guidance of the church leaders.

❏ *Screening will turn people off from serving*

> **Response.** Proper implementation and communication provide the answer to this concern. The focus should be upon providing a safe place for the youth and children of the church. Congregational members will rally around that objective. Some people may decline to serve, but consider the alternative of not screening.

❏ *This violates our trust in one another*

> **Response.** Just the opposite should occur. As members recognize that their church cares deeply about the welfare of the youth and children, their trust in church programs and their appreciation for the church's leadership will go up. They can have confidence that their church provides a safe and secure environment for youth and children. In whose custody would you prefer your children to be—in a church with an established and caring prevention program, or one where anyone can have access to your children? The key to promote trust is how the program is implemented and communicated to the congregation.

The cassette tape "What Church Leaders Should Know About Sexual Abuse and the Church" provides an excellent introduction to this issue for church leaders (see Appendix 7). Your church leaders can listen to the tape in their car as they commute to work or church. If possible, leaders should listen to the tape prior to the task force presentation. Finally, use segment one of the video tape (which is part of our prevention materials), as part of the presentation. At this point, church leaders must decide to take action. Assuming they agree to implement a prevention program, you are ready to move to the next step which will involve the initial formulation of program details.

3. Raise congregational awareness. Now that the decision has been made to establish a prevention plan, attention should be given to raising the awareness level of congregational members. The purpose is to inform the congregation of the key issues pertaining to child sexual abuse and why a decision has been made to establish a prevention plan. Begin to nurture an emotional commitment within your membership to develop a safe church environment for all children and youth.

To accomplish this goal, a communication strategy is needed. For example, designate one Sunday to introduce the issue. Develop a theme that will challenge and enlist people. A theme like, "Children—Our Most Valuable Possession" or "Responding to the Problem of Child Sexual Abuse" can be used. Since this issue touches people at a deep emotional level, careful planning should be done in advance. You may consider dismissing children prior to the sermon or a presentation on the topic. Recognition should be given that some members of the congregation may be adult survivors of abuse, and that you recognize the pain associated with this topic. The pastor may find a number of adults seeking counseling. Resources should be in place to respond to questions and personal needs that may surface in the days and weeks that follow.

The climate should be one of sober reflection but of hope. You want the people to realize that the church will be taking action to minister to this need. The focus should be upon the great responsibility God has given to us to care for our children. Scripture verses might be used such as the following: Psalm 78:1-6; Psalm 127; Psalm 46:1,6; 2 Samuel 13; Matthew 18:1-6; Matthew 18:10; Luke 18:15-17; Ephesians 5:11-13.

A good communication strategy will use several mediums to build support and understanding within the congregation. Consider using several of the following:

❑ Key note Sunday morning sermon

❑ Bulletin inserts (see samples in Appendix 6)

❑ Pastoral letter to members

❑ Newsletter article

❑ Special speaker or video for a combined adult education class

❑ Press release

❑ Posters in the church

70

❑ Special music or drama

❑ Educational seminar or workshop

Introducing the topic of child abuse and the prevention plan will create a variety of reactions among congregational members. Many will be in favor of the concept. Others will have questions and reservations. Provide opportunities for people to give feedback. The topic can also be discussed in small groups or home fellowships. Have staff members or other church leaders available who can answer concerns and provide specific answers about the church's plan.

4. Draft an initial policy. Once the *concept* receives approval, use Part Two of this book as a basis to formulate an initial policy statement. This process should occur simultaneously with your congregational awareness effort. Address the issues of worker selection, worker supervision, reporting obligations, and responding to allegations. Contact the appropriate community and state agencies as well as your insurance agent to obtain input and information. Solicit the input of ministry leaders and volunteer workers within the church. Create a sense of broad ownership for both the process and the policies that emerge as a result of your efforts. An attorney should review your policies to see that they conform to state law. Once congregational leaders approve the initial policies, you are ready for step 5.

5. Build consensus and revise policies if necessary. Meet with department heads and ministry leaders. Thoroughly discuss each policy and procedure. Work through all concerns. If problems exist in the policies, consider revisions, but do not sacrifice the integrity of the program. Work at developing a sense of unity before educating workers and volunteers.

6. Educate workers and volunteers. By now your workers should be well aware of the efforts to formulate a prevention plan. A strategy must be developed to train all existing workers. Once that has occurred, routines must be established for the training of all new workers who serve the church. Nursery workers fall into a category that we will consider separately.

A. Existing Workers. Schedule a mandatory training session for all existing staff, paid or volunteer, who work with youth or children. Since not everyone will be available, a second session should be offered on a different date. Prior to the session, distribute the policies and procedures, and the screening forms to the workers so they can read them prior to the meeting. At the training session focus on the following:

❑ Begin with a devotional including prayer

❑ Review the reasons why the church is implementing the program (Video segment one can be used for this session)

❑ Explain the new policies and procedures (Video segment two can be used for this session)

❑ Review the forms

❑ Explain implementation procedures including how the screening forms are to be completed and returned. Some individuals will need to use a primary screening procedure, while others may use a secondary procedure.

❑ Answer any final questions

❑ Conclude with prayer

During the session emphasize that you desire ongoing feedback. After the policies are implemented, recognize that some adjustments and fine tuning will be required. The session will take three to four hours to complete. Consider meeting on a Saturday morning and include lunch.

B. Future Workers. Often, new workers begin together as a group at the start of a new quarter or educational period. Sometimes, however, a new worker becomes active after a program has already begun. A plan must exist so that all workers receive proper training regardless of when they begin. Policy training should begin with a new member orientation class. All church members should be aware of basic policies concerning working with youth and children. A simple brochure can be prepared that outlines these policies. Group training should occur at the start of any new endeavor that includes children or youth. Individuals who begin at a later date should meet with a designated person to review the policies and procedures and to complete the screening form. Ideally, these workers should view the entire video presentation and read training materials, such as this book, that your church uses.

C. Annual Training. An ideal time for annual training is each Fall as school begins and church programs gear up for the new church year. Consider inviting a social worker to review with the staff reporting obligations and other needs related to abuse prevention.

D. Nursery. Many churches use hundreds of volunteer workers in their nursery programs. Many of these volunteers may only serve a few hours each year. The secondary screening procedure should be considered for these workers. Practically, difficulty may exist in getting all of these volunteers to attend your training sessions. As an alternative, consider preparing a special brochure just for nursery workers that explains basic nursery procedures (e.g., where to find supplies) and behavioral guidelines for attendants. The brochure can explain why a screening form is used. The nursery coordinator can see that each nursery worker receives the brochure and completes a secondary screening form prior to his or her service. These workers will already understand the procedure if it has been adequately explained during the new member orientation.

7. Monitor program progress. After the initial emphasis on the program wanes, workers may begin to ignore basic policies. For example, the two adult rule may become routinely neglected. Attention must be given to periodic monitoring that examines the following:

❑ Has each department trained its workers regarding these policies?

❑ Are workers following the required policies and guidelines?

❑ What obstacles exist in complying with the policies?

- [ ] What is the level of cooperation?

- [ ] Do sufficient materials exist for training and information?

- [ ] Are the policies printed and available?

Approximately six to eight weeks after implementation, give a written questionnaire to all ministry leaders and workers to gather additional feedback regarding these policies. Results of the monitoring process should be provided to the church board or committee responsible for the ongoing maintenance of the prevention effort. This group can then make recommendations for policy changes if necessary.

While complete enforcement of policies may not always be possible, screening procedures, reference checks and initial training must always be enforced.

8. Program evaluation. Church leaders should conduct an annual review of the prevention program. They should assess how well the program has met its goals. Ministry leaders can report on the prevention efforts. A brief questionnaire can be given to workers and representative church members asking for their reactions and concerns. Reports and anecdotes provide important sources of evaluation. The story of one child spared abuse or one worker cleared of allegations would speak highly of the value of the program. The evaluation becomes the basis for reviewing and improving the program.

On February 28, 1992, a 7-women, 5-man jury found the Catholic diocese of Sacramento not liable in an abuse case. Although the defendant, who was a church employee, was found guilty, the church was released from all liability because it took every reasonable caution.

References

Breach of Trust Breach of Faith: Child Sexual Abuse in the Church and Society. Publication services of the Canadian Conference of Catholic Bishops, 90 Parent Avenue, Ottawa, Ontario KIN 7B1

Conte, John R. *A Look at Child Sexual Abuse. National Committee for Prevention of Child Abuse.* Chicago, 1986.

Decree On Child Abuse: Policies, Procedures, and Recommendations. The Archdiocese of Cincinnati, 100 East Eight Street, Cincinnati, OH 45202, (513) 421-3131

Finkelhor, D., Hotaling, G., Lewis, I., and Smith., C. "Sexual Abuse in a National Survey," *Child Abuse and Neglect.* (14:19-28), 1990.

Fortune, M. Marie. "A Millstone 'Round the Neck," *Round Table* (Spring) 1990.

_____. *Sexual Violence: The Unmentionable Sin.* New York: Pilgrim Press, 1983.

Geffner, R. "Current Issues and Future Directions in Child Sexual Abuse." *Journal of Child Sexual Abuse.* Vol. 1 (1 1992).

Kendall-Tackett, K., Williams, L. and Finkelhor, D. Paper presented at the American Professional Society on the Abuse of Children, January 1991, San Diego, California 1991.

The Incidence and Prevalence of Child Sexual Abuse: No Easy Answer. National Resource Center on Child Sexual Abuse. Huntsville, AL,: 1992.

Sloan, I. *Child Abuse: Governing Law and Legislation* (1983).

The Cardinal's Commission on Clerical Sexual Misconduct With Minors (Chicago: Archdiocese of Chicago, June 1992).

The Report of the Winter Commission, Vol 1, 1990.

Wurtele, S., Kvaternick, M. and Franklin, C. "Sexual Abuse Prevention for Preschoolers: A Survey of Parent's Behaviors, Attitudes, and Beliefs." *Journal of Child Sexual Abuse* Vol. 1 (2: 113-127), 1992.

For additional information regarding the issue of child sexual abuse, contact:

The National Committee for Prevention of Child Abuse (NCPCA), 332 S. Michigan Avenue, Suite 1600, Chicago, Illinois 60690, (312) 663-3520.

The National Resource Center On Child Sexual Abuse, 107 Lincoln Street, Huntsville, Alabama 35801, 1-800-KIDS-006.

The Family Violence & Sexual Assault Institute, 1310 Clinic Drive, Tyler, Texas 75701, (903) 595-6600.

Appendix 1

Sexual Molestation: Victims And Perpetrators

victim	perpetrator	comments
pre-adolescent children ("pedophilia")	• adult male or female • adolescent male or female • clergy or lay workers • compensated or volunteer workers	• heterosexual or homosexual contact • fixated or repressed behavior • examples include molestation by Sunday School teachers, Christian school teachers, nursery and preschool workers, camp counselors, scout leaders, and adults who transport children to church or serve as "second fathers"
adolescent children ("ephebophilia")	• adult male or female • adolescent male or female • clergy or lay workers • compensated or volunteer workers	• heterosexual or homosexual contact • examples include molestation by youth pastors, volunteer "youth workers," Sunday School teachers, Christian school teachers, camp counselors, and scout leaders

Appendix 2

Primary Screening Form For Children Or Youth Work

© Copyright 1993 Church Law & Tax Report

Confidential

First Church

Note: Circled numbers correspond to explanatory notes immediately following the application.

① This application is to be completed by all applicants for any position (volunteer or compensated) involving the supervision or custody of minors. This is not an employment application form. Persons seeking a position in the church as a paid employee will be required to complete an employment application in addition to this screening form. It is being used to help the church provide a safe and secure environment for those children and youth who participate in our programs and use our facilities.

Personal

② Date _____

Name _____
         Last   First   Middle

③ *Identity must be confirmed with a state drivers license or other photographic identification.*
Present address: _____

City_____

State_____ Zip_____ Home phone (   ) _____

Please indicate the type of youth or children's work you prefer _____

Please indicate the date you would be available to begin _____

What is the minimum length of commitment you can make? _____

continued—page 1 of 4

④ Have you ever been convicted of or pleaded guilty to a crime?
___Yes (If yes, please explain—(attach a separate page, if necessary)_____

___No

⑤ Do you have a current driver's license?
___Yes   If yes, please list your drivers license number_____
___No

Church History and Prior Youth Work

⑥ Name of church of which you are a member: _____
List (name and address) other churches you have attended regularly during the past five years:

_____

_____

⑦ List all previous church work involving youth (list each church's name and address, type of work performed, and dates) _____

_____

⑧ List all previous non-church work involving youth (list each organization's name and address, type of work performed, and dates)_____

_____

List any gifts, callings, training, education, or other factors that have prepared you for children or youth work: _____

Personal References (not former employers or relatives)

Name _____   Name _____

Address _____   Address _____

Telephone_____   Telephone_____

continued—page 2 of 4

Applicant's Statement

⑨ The information contained in this application is correct to the best of my knowledge. I authorize any references or churches listed in this application to give you any information (including opinions) that they may have regarding my character and fitness for children or youth work. In consideration of the receipt and evaluation of this application by First Church, I hereby release any individual, church, youth organization, charity, employer, reference, or any other person or organization, including record custodians, both collectively and individually, from any and all liability for damages of whatever kind or nature which may at any time result to me, my heirs, or family, on account of compliance or any attempts to comply, with this authorization, excepting only the communication of knowingly false information.

I (check one):
❑ waive
❑ do not waive
any right that I may have to inspect any information provided about me by any person or organization identified by me in this application.

Should my application be accepted, I agree to be bound by the Bylaws and policies of First Church, and to refrain from unscriptural conduct in the performance of my services on behalf of the church.

I further state that **I HAVE CAREFULLY READ THE FOREGOING RELEASE AND KNOW THE CONTENTS THEREOF AND I SIGN THIS RELEASE AS MY OWN FREE ACT**. This is a legally binding agreement which I have read and understand.

⑩ Applicant's Signature _____.

Date

Witness_____

Date _____

continued—page 3 of 4

❶ Request For Criminal Records Check And Authorization

I hereby request the _____ Police Department to release any information which pertains to any record of convictions contained in its files or in any criminal file maintained on me whether local, state, or national. I hereby release said Police Department from any and all liability resulting from such disclosure.

_____
Signature

_____
Print name

_____
Print maiden name if applicable

_____
Print all aliases

_____
Date of birth

_____
Place of birth

_____
Social Security Number (if required by the Police Department)

_____
Today's date

Record sent to:

Name _____

Address _____

page 4 of 4

[Disclaimer: All forms in this book are for illustrative purposes, and under no circumstances should they be relied upon without the express, written advice of an independent and qualified attorney following a full legal analysis of all the circumstances. Neither Richard Hammar, Steven Klipowicz, James Cobble, Church Law & Tax Report, nor Christian Ministry Resources assumes any liability for reliance on this or any other form within this book.]

Explanatory Notes To Appendix 2

Note: The following explanatory notes correspond to the circled numbers on the sample form reproduced as Appendix 2.

① It is important for both volunteer and compensated workers to complete the application form. The form emphasizes, at the beginning, that its purpose is "to help the church provide a safe and secure environment for those children and youth who participate in our programs and use our facilities." This purpose should be emphasized continually in implementing a program to reduce the risk of sexual molestation or abuse. All completed forms should be kept in a locked file drawer.

② The form should be dated. This raises the question of whether or not the form should be updated periodically. By having workers complete this form when they are first hired, a church will reduce its risk of being sued for "negligent hiring" (assuming that references and previous churches are contacted, and questionable circumstances are investigated thoroughly). It is possible that a church could be sued for "negligent retention" for retaining such a person after it learns of information that call into question a particular worker's suitability for working with minors. Accordingly, the safest course of action would be to have all workers complete a screening form periodically (once every year or so). This practice has the additional benefit of taking advantage of changes in the screening form that are suggested by the most recent court decisions.

③ Photographic identification is essential to confirm the identity of any applicant whose identity is not known with certainty. Child molesters often use pseudonyms to prevent discovery of their criminal record.

④ One of the most important questions on the form. What kinds of criminal convictions disqualify an individual for youth work in the church? A criminal conviction for a sexual offense involving a minor would certainly disqualify an applicant. In the case of pedophilic behavior (molestation of a pre-adolescent child) such a conviction should disqualify an individual *no matter how long ago it occurred* (because of the virtual impossibility that such a condition can be "cured"). Other automatic disqualifiers would include incest, rape, assaults involving minors, murder, kidnapping, child pornography, sodomy, and the physical abuse of a minor. Other crimes would strongly indicate that a person should not be considered for work with minors in a church. Some crimes would not be automatic disqualifiers, because they would not necessarily suggest a risk of child abuse or molestation. Some property offenses would be included in this list, particularly if the offense occurred long ago and the individual has a long history of impeccable behavior.

⑤ The drivers license number of the applicant can be given to the church's insurance company, which can check on the applicant's driving record. This is a very important precaution to take with regard to anyone who will be driving children or youth in the course of church activities.

⑥ This information is needed to adequately check out the background and suitability of an applicant for children's or youth work. If an applicant is not a member of your church, or has been attending for only a brief period of time, it is very important to check with the churches the applicant has been attending for the past 5 years to determine his or her suitability for working with children and youth.

⑦ It is important to know if the applicant has worked with minors in any other church. If so, you should contact the other church to determine the applicant's suitability for working with children and youth.

⑧ It is important to know if the applicant has worked with minors in any other organization outside of the church . If so, you should contact the other organization to determine the applicant's suitability for working with children and youth.

⑨ This paragraph is very important in minimizing the legal liability of the church and any reference. The applicant (assuming he or she signs the form) (1) authorizes any reference or church listed in the form to provide information regarding his or her suitability for working with minors; (2) releases a reference from any liability for providing information about the applicant; and (3) may or may not waive the right to see any reference provided to the church regarding the applicant.

⑩ The applicant should sign the form in the presence of a witness who also signs the form. Alternatively, you may wish to have the applicant's signature acknowledged by a notary public.

❶ While every applicant or worker should sign this criminal records check authorization, this does not mean that the church should do a criminal records check on every worker. Rather, criminal records checks ordinarily should be viewed as an extraordinary procedure that may be desirable if questions are raised about a particular applicant or worker. The application should be completed by every applicant for any position involving the custody or supervision of minors. The application should also be completed by current employees or volunteers having custody or supervision over minors.

Should you ask if the applicant was a victim of abuse as a minor? A Supreme Court case in Alaska suggests that it may be negligent for a church to hire children's workers without asking them if they were themselves victims of child abuse. Some churches, in consultation with a local attorney, may choose to add a question about previous abuse. Persons who answer yes to such a question, or who leave it unanswered, should not automatically be disqualified from further consideration. Rather, this information simply imposes on the church a higher duty of care. This duty can be discharged in most cases simply by running a criminal records check on the individual. If it comes back with no record of any child abuse or molestation, or any other disqualifying crime, and if there is no other indication that the applicant poses a risk (from references or previous churches), then there is no reason why the person cannot be used.

In the alternative, the question could be asked during an interview of an applicant for children's or youth work. Churches should interview all applicants for children's or youth work prior to using them in any church program or activity. This question can be asked during the interview in lieu of asking it on the screening form. If the question is asked during an interview, it is essential for the church to use a standardized and written list of questions to be asked during an interview, and for this question to be one of the questions included on such a list. It is also important for the church to identify a person who will conduct these interviews, and for this person to be trained in the interviewing of children's and youth workers. Following the interview, there should be written notations on the interview form identifying the person who conducted the interview, the applicant who was interviewed, the date of the interview, and a summary of the applicant's responses to the questions. All information, whether collected on a form or during an interview should be kept strictly confidential.

Appendix 3

Reference Contact Form—Confidential

**Record Of Contact With A Reference Or Church
Identified By An Applicant For Youth Or Children's Work**

Copyright 1993 Church Law & Tax Report

Note: Circled numbers correspond to explanatory notes immediately following this form.

① Name of Applicant_____

② Reference or church contacted (if a church, identify both the church and person or minister contacted)_____

③ Date and time of contact _____

④ Person contacting the reference or church_____

⑤ Method of contact (e.g., telephone, letter, personal conversation) _____

⑥ Summary of conversation (summarize the reference's or minister's remarks concerning the applicant's fitness and suitability for youth or children's work)_____
_____
_____
_____

_____
Legible Signature

_____
Position

_____
Date

[Disclaimer: All forms in this book are for illustrative purposes, and under no circumstances should they be relied upon without the express, written advice of an independent and qualified attorney following a full legal analysis of all the circumstances. Neither Richard Hammar, Steven Klipowicz, James Cobble, Church Law & Tax Report, nor Christian Ministry Resources assumes any liability for reliance on this or any other form within this book.]

Explanatory Notes To Appendix 3

Note: The following explanatory notes correspond to the circled numbers on the sample form reproduced as Appendix 3.

① List the name and address of each reference you contacted. If you are reporting a contact with another church, list the name and address of the church you contacted, along with the name of the person you spoke with in the church. Be sure to prepare a contact summary for each reference or church you contact.

② Identify by name the person in your church who contacted the reference or the other church.

③ List the method used to contact the reference or the other church. Did you speak directly with the other person, use the telephone, or write a letter?

④ This is the most important information on the form. The person who contacted the reference or the other church summarizes the results of that contact. The ultimate question is whether or not the applicant is suitable for work with children or adolescent youth. The person contacting the reference or the other church should ask this question, and summarize the response on the form. If the person refuses to comment, be sure to note that on the form.

⑤ The person making the contact with the reference or the other church should sign the form, and list his or her position in the church. The date the form is completed should be noted.

⑥ Summarize the remarks made by the reference concerning the applicant's suitability for youth or children's work. If the reference has reservations about the applicant's suitability, be sure to note the facts that support the reference's reservations. Facts are of much more relevance than unsubstantiated opinions. Ask for the names of other persons who could verify the facts identified by the reference. For example, if the reference is aware of an incident of inappropriate contact with a child, were any witnesses present? Who were they? Some references may hesitate to provide you with information, particularly if it is negative. Read the applicant's statement at the end of the primary screening form. This authorizes the reference to comment on the applicant and releases the reference from liability for statements that are made.

Appendix 4

Secondary Screening Form Example

The disturbing and traumatic rise of physical and sexual abuse of children has claimed the attention of our nation and society. The following policies reflect our commitment to provide protective care of all children, youth, and volunteers who participate in church sponsored activities.

1. Adults who have been convicted of either child sexual or physical abuse should not volunteer service in any church sponsored activity or program for children or youth.

2. Adult survivors of childhood sexual or physical abuse need the love and acceptance of this church family. Individuals who have such a history should discuss their desire to work with children or youth with one of the pastoral staff prior to engaging in any volunteer service.

3. All adult volunteers working with youth or children are required to be members of First Church for a minimum of six months.

4. Adult volunteers should observe the "two adult" rule. This requires that adults are never alone with children or youth without an adult partner..

5. Adult volunteers should immediately report any behaviors which seem abusive or inappropriate to their supervisor.

Please Answer Each Question. Your Response Will Be Kept Fully Confidential.

1. As a church volunteer, do you agree to observe all church policies regarding working with youth or children?

___Yes
___No

2. Have you ever been convicted of or pleaded guilty to a crime? (see explanatory note ④ on page 80)

___Yes (Please describe on a separate sheet of paper)
___No

3. Were you a victim of abuse or molestation while a minor? (see explanatory note ⑤ on page 80)

___Yes
___No

If you prefer, you may refuse to answer this question, or you may discuss your answer in confidence with the senior minister rather than answering it on the form. Answering yes, or leaving the question unanswered, will not automatically disqualify an applicant for children or youth work. I have read the above policy and agree to observe the safeguards listed.

_____   _____
Signature   Date

_____
Please print name

Appendix 5

Sample Press Release Advocating An Abuse Prevention Program

The children of America are our country's most precious resource. The future hope of this nation rests upon their development and potential. Physical and sexual abuse endanger that future and shatter the innocence and purity of childhood.

Today, the ministerial association of Oak Grove announces a renewed commitment to confront this social problem. We call upon the churches and synagogues of our community, plus all other institutions that work with children and youth, to institute immediate safeguards to protect children and youth from physical and sexual abuse. As an association, we advocate the following policies and principles in an effort to provide a safe place for all young people within our community and beyond.

1. Child physical and sexual abuse are criminal actions which should not be tolerated in our society.

2. As a community we must work together to provide educational programs to instruct adults and children regarding the nature and impact of child abuse.

3. Victims of abuse need love, encouragement, and support. This extends not only to current victims, but to the many in our society who are adult survivors of childhood abuse.

4. All staff—paid and volunteer—who work with children should undergo appropriate screening. No adult who has been previously convicted of child abuse should work with children or youth.

5. At least two adults should supervise activities in which children or youth are involved. One of these should be an adult of at least 21 years of age.

6. No adult should spend unsupervised time alone with any child or adolescent without the awareness and consent of that individual's parents or legal guardians.

[Disclaimer: All forms in this book are for illustrative purposes, and under no circumstances should they be relied upon without the express, written advice of an independent and qualified attorney following a full legal analysis of all the circumstances. Neither Richard Hammar, Steven Klipowicz, James Cobble, Church Law & Tax Report, nor Christian Ministry Resources assumes any liability for reliance on this or any other form within this book.]

Appendix 6

Sample Bulletin Insert #1
(for use when introducing prevention program)
Safeguarding Our Children

Bob sat before Pastor Smith, slumped over in a posture of shame. His massive shoulders heaved as he tearfully shared the sad story. Over the last two years he has repeatedly molested his fourteen-year-old stepdaughter. This activity may have been kept from public awareness except that he molested another child, who was in the junior high school class that Bob taught. The child's complaint alerted the church staff and led to this painful confrontation. Pastor Smith listened, shocked and dismayed at the situation. He could hardly believe it—this could never happen here. Bob, a well respected business figure, church leader, husband, and father of two teenage boys, had committed child sexual abuse!

"This could never happen in our church." This might be your response when hearing about cases of child sexual abuse. It seems almost impossible that such a heinous activity could taint our community of faith. But it can. Incidents of child sexual abuse cut across every racial, social, economic, and religious boundary. This year alone, over one million children will be victims.

Often, we in the church have a false sense of a security about this problem. As a result, preventive steps may be neglected. Our common stereotypes often bolster this sense of security. The child molester is viewed as a predatory stranger who can easily be spotted by the church family. The sad truth is that 80 percent of child sexual abuse is perpetrated by someone the child knows and trusts . . . a parent, teacher, coach, and yes, a church youth worker.

Sexual abuse is devastating. It causes deep and sometimes lifelong psychological damage to the victim. The community reputation of a church is jeopardized. Reporters and mini-cam crews from the local news media will ensure that the scandal is well publicized. The church also becomes vulnerable to costly and time-consuming legal action. Jury awards of over a million dollars are commonplace and are often not covered by church insurance. Such indebtedness can cripple a church for decades!

First Church desires to be a safe place for all children who attend. We believe that preventive steps can be taken to promote the safety of children and those who volunteer to work with them.

First Church is adopting a needed prevention program to reduce the possibility of child sexual abuse occurring in this congregation. It will employ both education and new policies. Effective education will help make us aware of the nature of this problem. Prudent policies, proven successful in other situations, will be implemented to safeguard children, youth, and workers. These guidelines are available from this church. Please take time to read and familiarize yourself with this material. Let our "it could never happen" attitude become a "we won't let it happen here" one.

Bulletin Insert #2
(Introducing the topic area of child sexual abuse)
Stopping The Thief Of Childhood

A recent news story reported an attempted robbery in an inner city bank. The bandit easily obtained money from the cashier, but as he tried to escape, he was apprehended by an angry group of bank patrons who refused to allow him to get away with their savings. One police officer afterwards remarked that people could stop crimes if they would work together.

We in the church need to work together to stop another thief at large in our nation. This thief is shamelessly stealing the future potential of our children. The thief is child sexual abuse.

Child sexual abuse robs children of their innocence and dignity. It steals from them their chances of healthy emotional and sexual development. It robs them of trust in those they respect, and if this abuse occurs in church, it could rob them of their faith in God. The Church must not only recognize this thief, but band together with others who care to stop child sexual abuse.

Child sexual abuse or molestation occurs whenever an adult has sexual activity with a minor or youth. Sexual abuse creates emotional pain and confusion in its victims. It is always wrong and the young person is always the victim. In every state it is illegal and criminal.

Child sexual abuse is reportedly at epidemic levels. This year alone over 1,000,000 children and youth will be sexually abused. One in four families is affected by child sexual abuse. In over 80 percent of these tragic situations the children will be abused by someone they know and trust.

Although the majority of this abuse occurs within the home, over 30 percent of cases involve adults in day care, sporting, educational, and religious programs. Victims can be found among every social, racial, economic, and religious group in our nation.

In the weeks to come, we will join the fight against child sexual abuse in a more formal way. We are at an opportune and strategic place to help stop the "thief". Through a committed effort, God's people can provide a powerful voice of leadership to our society. We can begin now to turn the tide against this social ill by taking the following steps:

1. Educate ourselves as a community of faith about the problem of child sexual abuse.

2. Implement effective prevention programs within the church to create a safe place for all who attend.

3. Provide compassionate support and ministry to the large number of adult survivors of childhood sexual abuse. It is estimated that 1 in 4 adult women and 1 in 6 adult men have been abused before the age of 18.

4. Politically support actions that outlaw child pornography, prostitution and other types of child sexual exploitation.

In the weeks to come, you will being hearing more about the problem of child sexual abuse and how we in this church can begin to take specific steps to prevent this type of activity from harming children in our church and community.

Appendix 7

Description of Resources, Workshops, and Consulting Services to Help Churches Prevent Sexual Abuse and Other Risks

Employment Applications and Screening Forms

The following application booklets contain employment and screening forms exclusively designed for church use. Price: $3 per booklet. Instructional book available for $9.95.

❑ *Application Booklet for Church Employees*

❑ *Application Booklet for Volunteer Workers*

❑ *Application Booklet for Ministers*

The Informational Support Program (ISP)

Through ISP, a congregation can stay on the cutting-edge of every important legal and tax development that affects clergy and churches. The program consists of a network of vital resources directed to all levels of congregational life and leadership. **The regular price for these resources is over $160, but the program subscription fee as of the date of this text is only $89 per year plus $9 for postage and handling.** If desired, each individual resource can be ordered separately (the individual price is listed following each description). The resources include the following:

❑ *Church Law & Tax Report.* A bimonthly newsletter, Church Law & Tax Report provides detailed information and guidance on legal and tax developments as they occur. Each issue contains feature articles, a tax calendar, and updates on all recent legal and tax developments. Intended users include clergy, governing board, treasurer, bookkeeper, church attorney, and other church leaders. Price: $78 per year.

❑ *Church Leader Alert Tape Series.* This highly innovative and interesting tape series brings the insights and opinions of national leaders directly to your church board. Each tape focuses on liability issues that face local church leaders. Interviews with attorneys, insurance executives, local church leaders, denominational executives, and specialists in a variety of fields provides vital insights. Price: $22.95 for a two tape set.

❑ *Church and Clergy Tax Guide.* Updated annually, the Church and Clergy Tax Guide provides the most comprehensive information on federal taxation available today for both churches and clergy. What sets the Church and Clergy Tax Guide apart from other tax guides is not only its comprehensive treatment of subjects affecting churches and clergy, but its year-round value. Topics such as social security, retirement plans, charitable contributions, federal reporting requirements, housing allowances, designated offerings receive thorough treatment. The Church and Clergy Tax Guide is the one detailed reference book that will answer almost every question that a pastor or church treasurer will have over the course of the year on tax related issues. Price: $14.95.

❑ *Federal Reporting Requirements for Churches Cassette Tape—Annual Update.* Each December your church treasurer or bookkeeper will receive a step-by-step review of how to complete and file important forms with the federal government. Attention will be given to all important Forms such as 941, W-2, W-3, 1099 MISC, 1096, 8282, 8283 and 5578. Along with the next resource, your church treasurer or bookkeeper will have a personal continuing education program. Price: $9.95.

❑ *Income and Expenses for Church Workers Cassette Tape—Annual Update.* Determining what is income and how to handle expenses are two of the most problematic areas for churches today. Failure to properly determine income can create serious problems for both the church and its workers. This tape provides an annual update of all tax developments in these areas and helps church treasurers and clergy to take full advantage of the tax law in order to maximize the earnings of all church workers, and to eliminate potential problems for the church.Price: $9.95.

❑ *Clergy Filing Procedures Cassette Tape—Annual Update.* This tape provides step-by-step instructions in filing the federal tax forms that most clergy use. Attention is given to Schedule A, Schedule C, Schedule SE, Form 1040, Form 2106, and Form 1040 ES. Clergy will receive practical help regarding the complex and often confusing rules that apply to ministerial tax filing. Price: $9.95.

❑ *Annual Bulletin Insert.* ISP includes 200 bulletin inserts on an important topic relevant to your congregational members. For example, one popular insert is "What Every Congregational Member Should Know About Charitable Contributions" which is updated annually. Price: $15.90.

Sexual Abuse Prevention Resource Kit

This resource kit includes a training video and leader's guide, an audio cassette tape, and a resource book. The regular price for these resources is $58.85, but the kit fee is only $49.95. If desired, each resource can be ordered separately (the individual price is listed following each description).

❑ *Sexual Abuse Prevention Resource Kit.* Includes all of the following resources. Price: $49.95.

❏ *Training Video and Leader's Guide.* The first segment of the video helps church leaders and members understand why churches must take actions to reduce the risk of sexual abuse. Segment two covers the policies described in Part Two of this book. The tape comes with a leader's guide that provides detailed instructions on how to use the tape for training purposes. The tape and leader's provide important support in implementing a prevention program in the local church and are strongly recommended. Price: $39.95.

❏ *What Church Leaders Should Know About Sexual Abuse and the Church—Audio Cassette.* This tape helps church leaders understand how the problem of sexual abuse affects local churches and provides a powerful motivation to launch a prevention program. Price: $9.95.

❏ *Reducing the Risk of Sexual Abuse in Your Church—Resource Book.* Composed of three parts, this book provides detailed guidance on how to enlist the support of key leaders, formulate policies and procedures, and train workers. Price: $8.95.

Church Workshops and/or Consulting Services

Workshops and consulting services are available to assist local churches to implement a prevention plan. Workshops can include up to five participating congregations. Special arrangements can be made for denominationally sponsored events. Prices vary depending upon the number of participating churches. All workshops and consulting services are conducted by Church Law & Tax Report staff. For more information call Christian Ministry Resources at 1-704-841-8066.

❏ *Workshop 1—Launching A Prevention Program.* This workshop helps church leaders understand the importance of a prevention program and provides detailed guidance on launching a program in a local church. A typical format would include sessions on Friday night and Saturday.

❏ *Workshop 2—Training Church Workers.* This workshop provides training to church workers to reduce the risk of child or sexual abuse within the church. Attention is given to understanding the nature of abuse and procedures designed to protect both children and workers.

❏ *Consulting Service—Launching a Prevention Program.* The consulting service includes the Sexual Abuse Prevention Kit, plus 1 hour of telephone consulting in launching a program in your local church. Price: $125.

All prices are subject to change.
To order, write Christian Ministry Resources, PO Box 2301, Matthews, NC 28106, or call 1-800-222-1840.

GLOSSARY

child abuse: defined by state law , but generally includes (1) non-accidental physical injury, (2) sexual contact or exploitation, (3) neglect, and (4) emotional distress.In most states child abuse may be inflicted by an adult. However in some states, the definition of child abuse is limited to abuse inflicted by a parent caregiver.

child sexual abuse: defined by state law, but generally any sexual contact with or exploitation between an adult or caregiver and a child or adolescent even if the victim gives consent.

ephebophilia: an exclusive sexual interest in adolescents usually of the same gender.

exhibitionism: sexual perversion marked by a tendency of indecent exposure.

felony: a serious criminal offense as defined by state or federal law.

guarantor: a person or organization that is legally responsible for the actions or debts of another.

homosexual contact: in reference to child sexual abuse, this indicates the nature of the offense and not the sexual orientation of the offender.

liability: legal responsibility, often resulting in monetary damages.

molestation: improper sexual advances or activity with a child.

negligence: a failure to exercise reasonable care.

negligent selection: a failure to exercise reasonable care in hiring or selecting either paid employees or volunteer workers.

negligent supervision: a failure to exercise reasonable care in the supervision of either paid employees or volunteer workers.

pedophilia: an exclusive sexual interest in children who are before the age of puberty.

perpetrator: a person who commits an act of child sexual abuse

punitive damages: money damages that can be awarded by a court against a person or organization that engages in reckless behavior.

policy: a rule which describes or structures the proper working behavior of a church staff member or volunteer.

promiscuity: the tendency towards indiscriminate frequent sexual behavior.

reasonable care: the care that would be exercised by an ordinarily prudent person under the same or similar circumstances.

respondeat superior: a legal principle by which an employer is legally responsible for the negligence of its employees committed within the scope of their employment.

seduction: inducing another person to engage in sexual contact.

INDEX

About The Authors

Richard R. Hammar, J.D., LL.M., CPA is an attorney and CPA, specializing in legal and tax issues affecting churches and clergy. He is a graduate of the Harvard Law School, and attended Harvard Divinity School. He is the author of *Pastor, Church & Law,* the standard reference work on American church law; the *Church and Clergy Tax Guide,* the standard text on church and clergy taxes (published annually); and *The Church Guide to Copyright Law,* the only text addressing the application of copyright law to churches and religious organizations. The second edition of his book, *Pastor, Church & Law,* was selected as "book of the year" in 1992 by *Christianity Today's "Your Church"* magazine. He also serves as editor of *Church Law & Tax Report,* a bimonthly newsletter reviewing significant legal and tax developments affecting churches and clergy. In 1990, he was inducted into the National Association of Church Business Administration "Church Management Hall of Fame." He is a member of the Missouri and Illinois Bar Associations, the American Institute of Certified Public Accountants, and the Christian Legal Society. He has worked in his church's nursery for over 10 years, and teaches a fourth grade Sunday School class.

Steven W. Klipowicz, M.Div., Ed.D. (cand.) is the Associate Director of Christian Ministry Resources and the Director of Continuing Education for Church Law & Tax Report. He received his Master of Divinity degree from Trinity Evangelical Divinity School and was active in pastoral ministry for over fifteen years. He has done extensive work with abusive families and is currently completing his doctoral research at the University of Illinois where he is focusing his studies upon transformative learning in adulthood.

James F. Cobble, Jr., M.Div., D.Min, Ed.D. is the founder and Executive Director of Christian Ministry Resources and Publisher of *Church Law & Tax Report.* He received his Master of Divinity Degree from McCormick Theological Seminary and holds a Doctor of Ministry Degree from Princeton Theological Seminary. He also completed doctoral studies at the University of Illinois in Administration, Higher, and Continuing Education with a specialization in the continuing professional education of clergy. He is the author of *Faith and Crisis in the Stages of Life* and *The Church and The Powers.*